DIVIDED IRELAND

Bifocal Vision in Modern Irish Drama

Ronald Gene Rollins

UNIVERSITY
PRESS OF
AMERICA

LANHAM • NEW YORK •

Copyright © 1985 by

University Press of America,® Inc.

4720 Boston Way
Lanham. MD 20706

Library of Congress Cataloging in Publication Data

Rollins, Ronald Gene.
    Divided Ireland.

    Bibliography: p.
    1. English drama—Irish authors—History and
criticism.   2. English drama—20th century—History
and criticism.   3. Ireland in literature.   4. Politics
in literature.   I. Title.
PR8789.R65   1985   822'.91'099415   85-17856
ISBN 0-8191-4939-X (alk. paper)
ISBN 0-8191-4940-3 (pbk. : alk. paper)

All University Press of America books are produced on acid-free
paper which exceeds the minimum standards set by the National
Historical Publications and Records Commission.

To Tom, Nita, Malania and Tim

ACKNOWLEDGEMENTS

I am grateful to the following publishers for permission to quote
from publications which they control:

To the University of Toronto Press for a passage from Theatre and
Nationalism (1971) ed. Robert O'Driscoll. To The Sean O'Casey
Review for a passage from "Ideas and Ideology in The Plough and
the Stars" (1976) by Ronald Ayling. To Macmillan Publishing
Company, Inc. for the last stanza from "Easter 1916" from The
Collected Poems of William Butler Yeats (1959) by William Butler
Yeats. To Little, Brown and Company for passages from The
Collected Plays I-II (1960) by Denis Johnston. To St. Martin's
Press Incorporated for passages from Three Plays (1957) by Sean
O'Casey. To the Proscenium Press and The Journal of Irish
Literature for passages from "An Interview with Denis Johnston"
(1973) by Gordon Henderson. To the Proscenium Press for passages
from Joseph Holloway's Irish Theatre, I, II, III (1968) eds.
Robert Hogan and Michael J. O'Neill. To Indiana University Press
for a passage from "Myth: A Symposium" (1958) ed. T. A. Sebeock.
To Macmillan Publishing Company, Inc. for passages from Collected
Poems (1933) by William Butler Yeats, and for passages from
Collected Plays (1952) by William Butler Yeats. To Columbia
University Press for passages from The Tragic Drama of William
Butler Yeats: Figures In a Dance(1965) by Leonard E. Nathan. To
the Johns Hopkins University Press for passages from "Yeats' Last
Plays: An Interpretation" (1951) by Donald R. Pearce. To Uni-
versity of Toronto Press for a passage from "W. B. Yeats: Vari-
ations on the Visionary Quest" (1960) by Alex Zwerdling. To Holt,
Rinehart and Winston and CBS College Publishing for a passage
from Personality (1980) by Paul R. Abramson. To Humanities Press
Inc. for a passage from The Irish Drama of Europe from Yeats to
Beckett (1978) by Katherine Worth. To Farrar, Straus and Giroux
Inc. for passages from Philadelophia, Here I Come (1965) by Brian
Friel. To Atheneum Press for passages from Da (1978) by Hugh
Leonard. To Grove Press, Inc. for passages from All That Fall
(1981) by Samuel Beckett. To Farrar, Straus and Giroux for
passages from Crystal and Fox (1969) by Brian Friel. To Houghton
Mifflin Company for passages from Nature and Other Miscellanies
(1922) by Ralph Waldo Emerson. To Harcourt Brace Jovanovich for
passages from Shooting An Elephant and Other Essays (1950) by
George Orwell. To The Canadian Forum for passages from "Language
of Conquest, Language of Survival" (1982) by Michael Quigley. To
Faber and Faber Ltd. for passages from Translations (1981) by
Brian Friel. To the Stratford Shakespearian Festival Foundation
of Canada for passages from "The Dual Vision of Brian Friel"
(1982) by Ronald Bryden. Title modification suggested by Robert
Flanagan.

Table of Contents

Preface

As the title indicates this book is a collage--a collection of
diverse, critical comments--whose major purpose is to isolate,
accentuate and evaluate from odd angles and with different
degrees of light the abundance of configurations and crises, both
personal and communal, in eleven plays by six different play-
wrights--William Butler Yeats, Sean O'Casey, Denis Johnston,
Samuel Beckett, Hugh Leonard and Brian Friel--who, with different
degrees of patience and perception, follow their characters
across city streets, down country lanes and into some dark
interiors on a green, wet and rocky island, Ireland. A spectrum
of sorts, this short anthology attempts to capture part of
Ireland's radiant energy in a series of images or chapters, both
dispersing and sharply focusing the component waves of light--the
different struggles for love and understanding--into a pattern
revealing their different wave lengths, mass and energy--their
duration, size and intensity. If not a spectrum, then the book is
a revolving viewer with six glass panels that enables interested
individuals to look in upon the topography, texture and tumult of
a small nation struggling to know and define itself.

Written in part to answer questions raised by me and my students
in classes, chiefly undergraduate, at the University of Cincin-
nati, Marshall University, Ohio Wesleyan University and Trinity
College Dublin, these essays yoke by violence together eleven
plays (two in each chapter) from the reading lists for these
classes which exploit similar situations, symbols, sequences,
arguments, and characters, the assumption being that the study of
one work helps explain another. The last chapter is the one
exception to this arrangement as it is limited to a discussion of
one play, Friel's Translations. The headnotes preceding each
chapter are brief history lessons providing a minimum of historical and literary data relevant to the chapter's subject matter.

The first chapter, offering estimates of plays by O'Casey and
Johnston about the 1916 Easter Week insurrection, was first
published in The Sean O'Casey Review in 1977. The second essay
sorts out the duplication of mythical patterns in two plays by
O'Casey and was first published in Modern Drama in 1974. The
painful memories of old men in plays by Yeats and Beckett is the
subject of the third chapter, and this essay, revised and ex-
panded for this book, was first published in Eire-Ireland in
1978. The complex relationships between fathers and sons in plays
by Leonard and Friel is the subject for the fourth essay which is
being considered for publication. The shifting relationships
between two Irish odd couples in plays by Friel and Beckett is
the subject for the fifth essay, and part of this essay will
appear in Eire-Ireland in 1985. Finally, the destruction of an
Irish hedge-school by English progress as traced by Friel is the

subject for the sixth essay which will appear in <u>The Canadian</u>
<u>Journal</u> <u>of</u> <u>Irish</u> <u>Studies</u> in 1985.

Deliberately disjointed, this book, hopefully, approaches the
condition of "discordia concors", providing glimpses of
continuity and duplication amidst discontinuity and variation.
However, if some readers are annoyed by the absence of
transitional bridges linking the chapters, well, they may exert
themselves and build their own. If novelists like John Fowles can
ask readers for assistance in completing their books, then so can
critics. So it goes.

Ronald Rollins
Delaware, Ohio
February, 1985

CHAPTER ONE

PRELUDE

The Easter Rising, April 24-29, 1916

Easter Monday in Ireland on April 24, 1916 was a holiday and many
of Dublin's inhabitants were relaxing on the beaches, in Phoenix
Park and in the nearby Wicklow Mountains while others were at the
Fairyhouse Racecourse placing wagers on the different horses
running in the Irish Grand National. Other Irishmen--members of
the Irish Volunteers and the Irish Citizen Army--were not relaxing. Specifically, a large number of the latter group, led by
James Connolly and Padraic Pearse, seized the General Post Office
in Sackville Street shortly after noon and then came outside to
hear Pearse read a proclamation announcing the establishment of
an Irish Republic as a free and independent nation. Members of
the Irish Volunteers subsequently seized the College of Surgeons,
the Four Courts, the Imperial Hotel, Boland's Bakery and Jacob's
Biscuit Factory. The Easter Week Rising, to last five days with
450 killed and 2,614 wounded, had begun.

Isolating the two factors of vital importance to the success of
this uprising, Roger McHugh tallies the figures of the men and
women involved in this uprising, an insurrection that the sur-
prised British were at first inclined to view as a comic opera
revolution, another "cabbage patch" revolt like those of 1848 and
1867 in Ireland:

> The rising of 1916....depends on two things: the
> landing of a considerable quantity of arms from
> Germany and secondly a concerted rising of the Irish
> Volunteers which then numbered 12,000 men, combined
> with a rising of the few hundred men of Connolly's
> Irish Citizen Army. The first failed through the
> capture of the German arms ship, the Aud, and of
> Casement himself; the second because the commanding
> officer of the Irish Volunteers, on receipt of this
> news, cancelled the rising. But it took place because
> the extreme wing of the Irish Volunteers and of the
> Irish Republican Brotherhood had decided to go ahead
> in any case. In military terms this meant the confin-
> ing of the Rising to Dublin, instead of widespread
> fighting throughout the country; and that some 1,500
> men and 100 women opposed in Dublin some 2,500
> British troops which were increased to about 5,000
> within twenty-four hours. With 10,000 armed police
> (the Royal Irish Constabulary) to control the rest of
> the country it was a comparatively simple military
> operation to surround the few strong-points in the

Dublin occupied by the Republicans who, lacking
numbers and artillery, managed to hold out six days,
during which half the centre of Dublin was reduced to
ruins.[1]

Before the smouldering fires of devastated Dublin had time to
burn themselves completely out, General Sir John Maxwell, commander of British forces in Ireland, decided to teach the Irish
nation a convincing lesson about the folly of armed rebellion by
executing the leaders of this Irish alliance. Ignorant of Ireland's long tradition of respect and adoration for the many
martyrs who had died in her struggle for national survival,
Maxwell had Pearse and fifteen others executed over a two week
period. Also about 3,500 men and 79 women were placed under
arrest by British forces. As one might expect, this brutal
suppression quickly made heroes and martyrs of these Easter Week
rebels with their makeshift gray-green uniforms and slouch hats.
Ugly years of stealth, ambush, assassination, and intimidation
followed until the Irish Free State was established in 1921.

William Butler Yeats gives us his response to this insurrection
in "Easter 1916", a modified elegy written one year after the
event, that traces the Irish rebels' metamorphosis from red-faced
clowns in a casual comedy to permanent heroes of history, men who
will be remembered "wherever green is worn." AE (George Russell)
does likewise in 1932 in "Michael", a dream-vision poem isolating
Pearse as the very incarnation of the mythical Cuchulain. More
clear-eyed, critical, and ironic than Yeats or AE, Sean O'Casey
discloses his very different stance when he fashions his dramatic
documentary The Plough and the Stars in 1926, a quasi-history
play designed to broadcast selected passages from Pearse's public
declamations above the babble of the multitude, and to delineate
the devastation that must inevitably follow in the wake of those
committed to the mysticism of martyrdom and its attendant desire
for apotheosis via a tragic death. Carefully creating three rebel
warriors who shout the slogans of one segment of the Volunteers
and the Citizen Army, O'Casey deliberately limits his play's
focus so as to satirize the argument that Ireland should welcome
war as she would the Angel of God. As Ronald Ayling explains:

> The six signatories to the Proclamation of Easter
> Week....represented a coalition of widely different
> interests with only, perhaps, one major consideration
> in common: the desire to free Ireland from British
> rule as soon as possible by any means at their
> command. By choosing extracts from the speeches of
> only one of the leaders (and these extracts illus-
> trating only one aspect, albeit an outstanding one,
> of his thinking), it could be said that O'Casey was
> unfair to the interests and views of the other

leaders and their parties, and even to Pearse's own
political thinking as a whole. The fact that O'Casey
does concentrate on such narrow issues—which Irish
audiences ought to have known represented only one
side to a complex emotional and intellectual
situation—indicates that he wanted his criticisms to
be seen and assessed in specific, restricted terms.
The play was not to be interpreted as a blanket
condemnation of nationalism....In fact, by exposing
Pearse's particular kind of fanatic religiosity—his
vision of the need for a 'blood-sacrifice'—O'Casey's
criticisms sought to cleanse the nationalistic cause
of traits of Messianic mania rather than to undermine
nationalism per se.

Unwilling to permit O'Casey to remain as the one major dramatist-
interpreter of this memorable week in Irish history, Denis
Johnston gives us a different view of the rising in The Scythe
and the Sunset, a 1958 three act drama with a large cast that
finally resembles an open debate on Irish politics in particular
and historical cycles or epochs in general. Unlike O'Casey,
Johnston gives equal time to the Irish and the English, and he
involves the Irish leader Tetley and the English officer Palliser
in a verbal fencing match—a match punctuated by sarcastic
badinage—that reminds one of similar situations from Shaw's
plays looking at love, politics, and revolution. Moreover,
Johnston's women are very different from O'Casey's, and Johnston's Emer only serves to remind us that women like Countess
Markiewicz and Maud Gonne were passionately involved in the
dangerous dynamics of Irish political and economic agitation.

Chapter One

O'Casey and Johnston: Reactions to the 1916 Easter Rising

> I write it out in a verse-
> MacDonagh and MacBride
> And Connolly and Pearse
> Now and in time to be,
> Wherever green is worn,
> Are changed, changed utterly:
> A terrible beauty is born.
>
> W. B. Yeats, "Easter 1916"

Violent social convulsions like the 1916 Easter Week Rising in
Ireland have frequently inspired works of art, jolting the
artist-observer's composure and forcing him to develop a height-
ened awareness--a clearer conception--of the public event and the
personalities, major and minor, who were participants, voluntary
and involuntary, in the hazardous activity. Sometimes the artist
sees the uprising as both a symptom of and the inevitable outcome
of the militant madness that pervades his particular country
or--as Denis Johnston regarded the 1916 insurrection--as but a
minor spasm in the historical twitchings that erode and fragment
one empire--one culture--to make way for another. Thus as he
cogitates about men resorting to violence to achieve their goals,
the artist begins to reshape and rearrange this particular event
in the crucible of his creative imagination. Certain incubating
ideas and motifs began to emerge and to jostle each other until--
through transformation and synthesis--the fascinated artist
fashions a sequence of ironic, symbolic, and iconic tableaus.
Struggling to blend different kinds of discernment and balance--
the revelry of comedy and the anguish to tragedy--the artist
gradually imposes his patterns upon the revolutionary action.
Ultimately a form is fashioned that is both argumentative and
evocative, possessing sometimes the universality of myth. Hence a
masterpiece is sometimes written in immediate or belated response
to a significant historical event.

Sean O'Casey's The Plough and the Stars is just such a masterpiece, an expansive four act dramatic documentary about the 1916
Easter Rising by a man who had been actively engaged in the
revolutionary trauma of Ireland. Imprisoned but later released
unharmed during the Rising, O'Casey was to brood about this
abortive rebellion for a decade; then came his masterpiece in
1926. Another lesser masterpiece inspired by O'Casey's play--and
the Rising itself--is The Scythe and the Sunset by Denis Johnston, another Irishman who was likewise held captive for three

4

days during this insurrection (members of de Valera's battalion
seized and barricaded his home) but who emerged unharmed and
amused to go on and become a successful playwright. Johnston
explains his reaction to Easter Week and O'Casey's play:

> As far as I am aware, only one other play about 1916
> was performed prior to my own, in spite of all
> impressions to the contrary....The other Easter Week
> play is, of course, Sean O'Casey's finest piece of
> writing, The Plough and the Stars--the play of which
> the title of mine is an obvious parody. Herein any
> intentional similarity ends, as it would be the act
> of an idiot for any dramatist to measure his play
> against such a yardstick as The Plough....Neither in
> verbiage, plot nor sentiments does this play of mine
> presume to bear any relation to its magnificent
> predecessor. The only point in so titling it lies in
> the fact that The Plough is essentially a pacifist
> play, implying that if only man had a 'titther o'
> sense,' these outbreaks of destruction and bloodshed
> would not occur. As a quiet man who, nevertheless, is
> not a pacifist, I cannot accept the fact that,
> theatrically, Easter Week should remain indefinitely
> with only an anti-war comment, however fine.[3]

Johnston is correct when he argues that his The Scythe and the
Sunset, a witty, Shavian debate drama where agile-minded, articulate people are clearly identified with definite ideological
commitments, is quite different from its impressive predecessor
with regard to language and plot, but he is short-sighted when he
contends that The Scythe and the Sunset does not echo some of his
sentiments--ideas--found in The Plough and the Stars. A careful
examination of both plays, while identifying the very great
differences, will reveal that the attitudes of the two playwrights regarding the motivation and conduct of men in conditions
of crisis are virtually identical.

Perhaps we might begin by observing that the casts of both plays
are relatively large and diversified, with Johnston's people
coming mostly from the middle and upper classes, and O'Casey's
from the lower. The range is great as we meet a professional
doctor who quotes Yeats and flirts with young women at one
extreme and a consumptive, lonely slum child at the other. Dr.
Myles MacCarthy is the whiskey-sipping, cynical doctor from the
Jarvis Street Hospital for mental patients in Johnston's play,
and Mollser is the tubercular fifteen-year-old child in
O'Casey's. Ranged in between these two extremes are the following: seven members of the Irish military with Commandant
Clitheroe, Captain Brennan, and J. Williams representing the
Irish Citizen Army, and Lieutenant Langon, Commandant Sean

5

Tetley, Liam O'Callaghan, and an unnamed man representing the
Irish Volunteers. Johnston introduces us to two English officers
in Captains Clattering and Anthony Palliser, the experienced,
professional soldier, in his play, while O'Casey uses two English
enlisted men--Sergeant Tinley and Corporal Stoddart--in his work.
Johnston has only one working girl in his play, Roisin, while
O'Casey shows us a street fruit-vendor, Bessie Burgess, a char-
woman, Mrs. Gogan, a wife of a bricklayer, Nora Clitheroe, and a
prostitute, Rosie Redmond. Johnston's other woman, Emer, is an
educated, well-dressed revolutionary who, unlike O'Casey's women,
conspires to keep the fires of revolution burning.

There is no one in O'Casey's play quite like Johnston's Endymion,
an ex-mental patient who injured his head while trying to rescue
a friend from drowning in a large vat in a Guinness brewery,
although Peter Flynn, Nora's vain uncle and a laborer fond of
outlandish dress, reminds one--especially when dressed to attend
a torch-lit procession--of Endymion. Flynn's fellow members of
the Dublin working world include the Young Covey, a fitter,
Fluther Good, a carpenter, and an unnamed Bar-Tender. The one
remaining member of O'Casey's cast is The Figure in the Window
whose appearance is so vital to O'Casey's satiric intent in Act
II. Thus the twenty-six members in the two casts form a recognizable cross-section of Dublin society, including both the high
and the low.

The Irish Must Save Face

If the casts are different, the plays' major thematic concerns
are not. Remembering how the Sinn Fein Volunteers were viewed
with widespread contempt by the majority of the Irish people
before the Easter Rising, Johnston suggests that it was this
"contempt"--not deeply-felt political or economic motives--that
drove the majority of the Irish rebels into action: "'Face', not
slogans, is one of the most powerful motivating forces in the
breasts of men, and these men had to prove that they were
soldiers, or disband in the face of ridicule."[4]

It is this torment in the face of ridicule from his sweetheart
Roisin that causes Michael Maginnis, Johnston's slow-witted,
obedient, emblematic Irish rebel who wonders why his fickle
countrymen label him a "Flyboy Fusilier" when he is inactive but
a "murderin' blaggard" when he is, to join the fighting with
C Company, Third Batallion at the end of Act I. Unwilling to be
called a renegade by Emer or to be scorned by Roisin, who wants a
Galahad in shining armor, Maginnis plunges into the fray, subsequently experiencing a strange metamorphosis which makes him

unable to "reckernize meself." One of the seven Irishmen confronting "hundreds" of Englishmen, Maginnis covers himself with
"dirt and glory," cooling his red-hot rifle with oil from a tin
of sardines. Routing the British at Ballsbridge, he returns to
receive a hero's welcome: a cigarette from Emer, a drink of stout
from Dr. MacCarthy, and looks of intense admiration from Roisin
who can't believe that mere "flesh and blood" could withstand
such extreme pressure.

It is this same issue of saving face that prompts the complicated
maneuverings--extended games of verbal fencing--between Anthony
Palliser, an Irishman serving as a captain in the English army,
and Sean Tetley, an English-Irishman (his father was an English
NonConformist who came to Ireland to manufacture rosary beads)
serving as commandant for the Irish Volunteers. Tetley, a quiet,
clean-shaven man in his thirties with a resolute jaw and "far-
away eyes," is a dreamer who is convinced that now is the time to
strike because the ranks of the Volunteers are thinning and
because the British face a major challenge with the Huns in the
Great War in Europe. Determined to see that his generation does
not go down in history as "craven" as the last, Tetley is proud
of his comrades' courage as they "take on" the British Empire in
open warfare for the first time in three generations, blaming
their failures and incompetence on ignorance of military tactics.

Yet this man dedicated to a dream--to a heroic cause that will
give "meaning" to his life--has his moments of introspection and
profound self-doubt. In Act I, he pauses to tell Emer: "I'd fight
to the last building and the last man if I was sure of only one
thing--that I was fighting for my country and for my people, and
not just for my own satisfaction."[5] Worried like T. S. Eliot's
Becket in <u>Murder in the Cathedral</u> about committing the right
action for the wrong reason, Johnston's Tetley worries about the
"derision" and the "murderous" laughter of the Irish who largely
ignored the reading of the Proclamation of Independence at the
start of the rebellion. So as his mood changes from hope to
despair as the English begin to converge on the rebel positions,
Tetley asks himself: "Do I have to pretend to myself that I'm
another Jesus Christ--that everyone's wrong except me?"[6]

Then his mood alters again as he reflects on how Roisin quickly
reversed her attitude toward Volunteer Maginnis, the impulsive
tram-worker hero. Perhaps the entire Irish nation would behave in
a similar manner if fifteen or twenty Irish rebels were to
receive their "just deserts". Knowing that the new British
commander is a severe man with a reputation as a hangman, Tetley
decides to surrender to the English and achieve martyrdom, but
only after giving Captain Palliser, his wounded prisoner in the
Pillar Cafe, his freedom.

Yet it isn't that simple because Palliser refuses Tetley's offer. Palliser will not walk or run to his freedom, serving as a Judas for Tetley-Jesus, the Irish leader and redeemer bent on crucifixion; he will not be a witness to Tetley's "apotheosis". It is then that Tetley discovers that Palliser is also excessively concerned with saving face, with demonstrating that the English also know how to confront danger and die. Irritated earlier by Emer's "invincible arrogance" about the Irishman's ability to face death and her desire to create a "holocaust" so that Tetley can win his "crown" of martyrdom, Palliser impulsively rigs the machine gun, which Tetley had carried into the cafe from the G.P.O., so that the Irish amateurs can end their "fantastic pantomine" and fight in a real war. When Emer promptly fires it into the midst of the Irishmen and Englishmen discussing peace terms near the O'Connell Monument, Palliser knows that he has been tricked into playing the other fellow's game. As he says, the "Book of Revelation" has been opened.

When later charged by Tetley with "showing off" by rejecting Tetley's offer of freedom to remain in the cafe that is directly opposite the G.P.O. and doomed to destruction by the fire, Palliser calmly replies that "other people....understand as much about death" as the Irish. Amazed, Tetley replies:

> And this is the fellow who had the nerve to call me
> pompous for knowing my own mind. I would never have
> believed in such vanity. But don't think that you can
> bully me out of my destiny. I warn you that if you
> insist, I shall leave you this bonfire for whatever
> satisfaction you can get from it.[7]

Tetley subsequently departs but only after admitting that Palliser has defeated him as he (Tetley) will defeat the English general. Thus the play's resolution underscores Johnston's belief that "men do not act from logical motives as often as they act under the promptings of the urge that I mentioned before--this thing that the Orientals call 'face'."[8]

These same unrehearsed mental and physical improvisations to save face also occur in The Plough and the Stars which also implies that men go to war--not for clearly defined political or economic reasons--but for personal ones, a desire to achieve personal renown. Certainly Jack Clitheroe, the I.C.A. solider who sulks like a schoolboy when he thinks his promotion has been denied him, is not depicted by O'Casey as a thoughtful rebel leader dedicated to a political cause, the liberation of his country. Rather, Clitheroe emerges as a histrionic and egocentric rebel jealous of his rivals in the military and inordinately proud of his I.C.A. uniform. Remembering Clitheroe's love of military attire and his feud with the I.C.A., Mrs. Gogan comments:

Just because he wasn't made a Captain of. He wasn't
goin' to be in anything where he couldn't be con-
spishuous. He was so cocksure o' being made one that
he bought a Sam Browne belt, an' was always puttin'
it on an' standin' at th' door showing it off, till
th' man came an' put out th' street lamps on him.
God, I think he used to bring it to bed with him![9]

But the real confrontation which isolates Clitheroe's vanity--his
foolish pride in keeping up false appearances--occurs in Act III.
Determined to prevent her husband from being "butchered" as a
sacrifice to the Fenian dead, Nora spends a night in desperate
search for her husband, a search which involves her in a fight
with a hussy at a street barricade who rails at Nora for reflecting shame on her husband and the women of Ireland by her "cowardly" action. With indignation Nora tells Mrs. Gogan that she saw
"fear glowin'" in the eyes of the rebels at the barricade in
North King Street, adding that the Irish rebels were "afraid to
say they're afraid."[10]

Jack subsequently demonstrates that he is one of these frightened
rebels unwilling to admit to his terror. When he returns to the
tenement with Captain Brennan, who is supporting the wounded
Lieutenant Langon near the end of Act III, Jack is momentarily
reunited with his joyful wife who is thankful to God that her
husband has been spared a bloody death. At first Jack admits that
he is sorry that he ever left his "beautiful Nora", but when
Brennan yells at Jack for "dallin'" with Nora while Langon dies
in his arms, Jack begins to reject Nora in favor of his comrades.
Then when he learns the details of Nora's search for him at the
barricades, he is visibly angry because he is worried that "her
action would give him future shame."[11]

What possessed you to make a show of yourself, like
that?....What way d'ye think I'll feel when I'm told
my wife was bawlin' for me at th' barricades? What
are you more than any other woman?[12]

When Nora defends her action by asserting that she was "mad with
terror", Jack quickly replies that she is going to turn all the
risks that he is taking into a "laugh". The heated exchange
continues when Brennan asks Jack if he is arranging for "another
honeymoon", a remark which infuriates Jack who protests savagely
that he is not a "renegade". Increasingly furious, Jack finally
loosens Nora's grip and pushes her away, but not before Nora
reminds both men of the truth they refuse to face:

Look, Jack, look at th' anger in his face; look at
th' fear glintin' in his eyes....He himself's afraid,
afraid, afraid!....He wants you to go th' way he'll

9

have th' chance of death strikin' you an' missin'
him!....His very soul is cold....shiverin' with the
thought of what may happen to him....It is his fear
that is tryin' to frighten you from recognizin' th'
same fear that is in your own heart![13]

Determined to prove to Nora, Brennan, and others that he is no
cowardly renegade afraid to face death, Jack, rejecting his
wife's entreaties, returns to the fighting and is killed in the
inferno that engulfs the Imperial Hotel. An inordinately vain and
foolish man and a reluctant hero, Jack dies because--like Johnston's soldier--he must save face. So Jack's hubris is truly a
high, reckless, arrogant pride, a vanity much like that detected
by Tetley in Palliser, who also dies in a flaming building.
Viewed by his Nora, Bessie Burgess, and others as a fool, Jack is
understandably praised by the General of the I.C.A.: "Commander
Clitheroe's end was a gleam of glory."[14]

Robot-Orator Paces and Preaches

Yet not all of the fighters who march through the two plays are
sunshine soldiers, false patriots with private dreams of heroic
selfhood. The Man in the Window is the dedicated revolutionary in
O'Casey's drama, a zealot who insists that the shedding of blood
helps a nation experience both a catharsis and a redemption. With
his jingoistic utterances and his deliberate walk, the Figure
seems unnatural and mechanistic, a robot-orator mesmerized by his
vision of a holy war leading to national liberation. With his
pleas that the Irish "rejoice" in war and willingly spill "red
wine" in "glorious sacrifice", the Figure is as drunk with his
dream as the pub-crawlers are with theirs. His demands are out-
rageous and O'Casey appropriately undercuts him for his obsessive
worship of war. Yet O'Casey also respects the "madness" of this
man who is willing to become a martyr; with his unswerving
commitment to his cause, the Figure, like Pearse before him, is
willing to sacrifice himself to attain a larger objective.
Reminding his listeners of the "Fenian dead" in Ireland's past,
the Figure argues that slavery is more horrible than bloodshed.
With his patriotic religiosity the Figure, then, is elevated,
both literally and symbolically, above his audience, a dreamer
surrounded and misunderstood by drunkards. O'Casey's remarks
about the vain patriots and the sincere Pearse are helpful:

But the "Orator" is not vain; he is dangerously
sincere: so sure that he is ready to kill or be
killed for his ideal, as many great men were--
Washington, Lincoln, Kosciusko. I knew this 'Orator'

well--Padraic Pearse, and there were none more
charming, gentle, or brave than he.[15]

Interestingly, this Figure appears four times to interrupt and
punctuate the progression of the Act II, and these carefully
spaced appearances remind us of the periodic arrival of a beam of
light from a lighthouse, a beam that enters to illuminate the
chaotic pub world of prostitute and patriot. Notice that each
time the beam enters, we see the pub's interior and its inhabitants in a different light. After his first appearance, when the
Figure argues that arms in the hands of Irishmen is a glorious
sight, we focus on the Barman who wishes he were younger so that
he could plunge "mad" into the middle of it, and on Peter Flynn
with a glass--not a gun--in his hand. Peter later exclaims that
the Figure's remarks made him "burnin'" to draw his sword, an
oversized toy which he handles in a clumsy manner. After the
Figure's second appearance, when he speaks of lives given gladly
for love of country, we get glimpses of hate and discord as the
Covey rejects prostitute Rosie Redmond's advances and taunts
Peter, and as Bessie slanders Mrs. Gogan and complains that Irish
soldiers won't fight to protect Catholic Belgium. Further, Bessie
rejects the Figure's idea that young lives should be "gladly"
given for a nation's freedom, adding that she is angry when she
thinks of the many Tommies (perhaps her own son) being torn into
bloody pieces on the earthen altar erected for the sacrifice of
heroes in Europe.

When the Figure appears for the third time, he contends that
Ireland has not known the exhilaration of war for one hundred
years. The pub inhabitants, increasingly frenzied in their
talking, drinking, and gesturing, respond by starting their own
war, a shouting match between Mrs. Gogan and Bessie who sends
Peter flying with an angry shove. Mrs. Gogan's baby is tempo-
rarily abandoned on the pub floor in the midst of this cursing
and scuffling. The Barman halts the war by pushing the two women
toward the door but more violence seems imminent when the drunken
Fluther discards his coat and hat to shadow box before the
delighted Rosie. Finally, when the speaker appears for the fourth
time, he insists that Ireland "unfree" will never know peace. The
excited I.C.A. men and Volunteers who subsequently enter confirm
his diagnosis as they shout imprisonment, wounds, and death for
the independence of Ireland.

Tetley is the sincere but troubled political idealist in The
Scythe and the Sunset, and he also repeats some of the ideas of
Pearse. As Johnston explains:

> My lack of personal knowledge of any of the leaders
> is my principal reason for not presuming to depict
> any of them by name, or even by implication, on the

11

stage. Nevertheless there is a certain similarity
between what one hears of the views and militant
idealism of Pearse and some of those expressed by my
character Tetley.[16]

Like Pearse, Tetley is a sensitive and compassionate man, an
introspective leader who broods about Ireland's past and future--
"the seven hundred years of history"--who suffers vicariously
with his comrades, and who is tenacious and resourceful in his
planning to conceal the incompetence of the rebels. As he
affirms: "What matters to me is that this week he turned from a
disgrace into a triumph."[17] Fascinated by brave men afflicted
with doubt and deficient in technical training, Johnston gives
us, therefore, a slight reflection of Pearse in Tetley, a man
more humane and approachable than the striding-speaking silhouette of O'Casey.

Predictably it is the women who respond in different ways to the
arguments from the Pearse figures that sacrifice is both necessary and glorious in war. Nora Clitheroe summarizes O'Casey's
convictions when she insists that no woman willingly "gives a son
or husband to be killed" in conflict; to do so would be a lie
against "God, Nature, an' against themselves."[18] Yet Johnston's
Emer is decidedly different, a patriotic fanatic excited and
energized by the possibilities of armed conflict. Ironically
named after Emer, wife of Cuchulain, a great hero of the Red
Branch Cycle of Irish tales, she is a calculating female, a
handsome, earnest-looking woman in her late twenties who wears a
green tunic and shirt. Channeling her unspoken love for Tetley
into revolutionary activities, Emer shows scorn for the Irish
rabble who loot the shops and stores in The Scythe and the
Sunset. Insisting that law and order must prevail if the
Provisional Government is to survive, Emer vigorously opposes
Williams' plan to ask the English for terms of surrender.
Convinced that the Irish rebels' conduct will change the
attitudes of the Irish people from cynical mockery to true
belief, she also opposes Palliser's efforts to save Tetley's
life; she wants his life to have a glorious end and thus achieve
"meaning". She does not hesitate to fire the stolen machine gun
once it is rigged, an action which is difficult to reconcile with
her self-appointed role as volunteer nurse wearing a Red Cross
apron. Even Roisin, who initially has some reservations about
killing, can't control her amazement at this nurse who fires a
gun so that she can drive "men to slaughter in the flames." Thus
Johnston is correct when he points out that his women are
different from O'Casey's:

    So also, it may be noticed that the mouthpiece for
    most of O'Casey's pacifism is provided by his women,
    whereas in actual fact the women of Ireland, ever
    since the Maud Gonne era, have been the most vocal

part of its militancy. If I can claim nothing else, I
can at least point with some complacency to the fact
that--when it comes to the point--both my women are
killers.[19]

Aside from Emer, dreaming of a new flag above the G.P.O.,
Endymion, Johnston's zany and one-man show, is perhaps the most
interesting figure in The Scythe and the Sunset. A former mental
patient of Dr. MacCarthy's Little Flower Refuge for Nervous
Complaints, he is a "fantastic figure" who wears an old-fashioned
bowler hat, a high collar and an eyeglass, a long-skirted sports
coat, and trousers tucked into his leggings: he also carries a
bundle of sticks, umbrellas, and a sword in a scabbard, all tied
together with red tape. Describing himself as a "chorus to these
large events" that will burn Dublin to the ground, Endymion is
the wise fool, the jester who speaks both sense and nonsense.
Explaining the play's title, Endymion predicts that when the
English ministers and generals arrive, Ireland will experience a
"bloody sunset from the east" as the man with the scythe, the
Grim Reaper, levels his harvest.

The World Is Upside Down

As the bedlam continues, Endymion places a pair of celluloid
cuffs on his ankles to indicate that the world is "upside down".
Observing that the Green makes murder and the Crown makes
martyrs, Endymion repeats Shakespeare's King Lear's "I will be
the pattern of patience".[20] His last appearance in Act III
involves a prophesy of the grim end of the Rising. Finishing his
dignified minuet with an invisible partner, Endymion notices that
the English are enjoying their "last days of power" and that
bunting shall soon hang in "gaunt cathedrals". Concluding that
the Irish are tired, "beyond all thinking", of themselves, he
retreats from Palliser's piano music, leaving the Irish and the
English to play the other fellow's game. Lacking Endymion's
"madness", O'Casey's Peter Flynn rivals his dress. With his
forester's uniform--green coat with gold braid, frilled shirt,
white breeches, top boots, slouch hat with white ostrich plume,
and sword--Peter would make an appropriate partner in Endymion's
mad minuet.

Fusing the "mad" prophesies of Endymion and The Figure in the
Window, O'Casey and Johnston thus translate history into reality
in their dramatic distillations of the 1916 Rising. Describing
his play as "an antimelodrama on what has now become a sacred
subject," Johnston perhaps speaks for both playwrights when he
adds that "Most plays about national uprisings are based upon an

13

assumption that the embattled rebels are always romantic and that the forces of oppression are totally wrong."[21] Rejecting these "shopworn axioms," both O'Casey and Johnston refuse to create black and white caricatures or puppets as patriots. Rather they fashion men of flesh and blood with recognizable human failings, and they both show that the Rising was, indeed, much a matter of playing the other fellow's game. Both dramatists are especially successful in their efforts to trace the jubilation, the confusion and the vacillation, both in thought and deed, that were apparently the distinguishing features of this insurrection. Certainly both anti-heroic works accent the playwrights' bias that men do not always behave rationally and compassionately in a public crisis of some significance, a crisis endangering the lives of many people, civilian and military. Rather, in manners appropriate to their imaginative genius, O'Casey and Johnston clearly stress their conviction that it is the vanity of men-- call it pride, self-esteem, or face--which figures so forcefully in the success or failure of any human enterprise, large or small. Such are the different reactions to a turbulent week in Irish history, O'Casey responding with a four act tragi-comic chronicle that is both musical and slightly distorted, and Johnston with a three act debate drama distinguished by witty conversation and sudden reversals of action.

PRELUDE

Myth in Modern Literature

In 1918 Jane Ellen Harrison published Themis, a study of the
origins of Greek mythology which argued that Greek myths evolved
out of earlier rites, these myths later appearing in modified
forms in religion, literature and art. Building on her
discoveries later anthropologists, psychologists and scholars
suggested that myth formed the matrix out of which literature
evolves, the characters, conficts, themes and icons of literature
being nothing more than the altered modifications of these very
same variables so visible in the world's enduring myths. In 1920,
for example, Jessie Weston developed the idea in From Ritual to
Romance that the Grail romances were disguised fertility rite
narratives. In 1949 Francis Ferguson demonstrated that the ritual
patterns of Sophocles' Oepidus Rex provided much of the basic
design for some modern plays. And in 1951 C. L. Barber traced the
Saturnalian patterns in Shakespeare's comedy, again linking
literature with myth and myth with ritual.

Less concerned with the origin of myths, modern writers have
integrated mythical materials in their work for different
reasons. D. H. Lawrence, for example, exploits the scapegoat myth
in "England, My England" so that he can contrast modern with
ancient culture, the modern culture engaging in sacrificial
murder for the defense of territorial rights and not community
cleansing. James Joyce uses Greek myth in Ulysses because it
gives him design and because it enables him to suggest something
about the sameness of the human condition. And John Fowles uses
Greek myth in The Magus because two ancient narratives provide
him with the prearranged sequence he needs to develop the
character and career of Nicholas Urfe, the selfish Englishman who
needs to be trained in the art of relating to and loving others,
especially women.

Sean O'Casey has some similar--and different--reasons for using
mythical material in two plays from the middle and late phases of
his long career. In Within the Gates he writes an ambitious
modern morality play crowded with archetypal figures but his real
subject is the destiny of the Young Woman who is pulled in one
direction by the Bishop and in another by the Dreamer, a resur-
rection of the old morality play arrangement. To bestow additional dimensions of meaning upon the Young Woman (and to provide
insight into her internal debate), O'Casey associates through
dress Jannice with Janus, the Roman god identified with gates and
beginnings in that ancient world. O'Casey's objective in using

15

mythical materials in his other play, <u>Cock-A-Doodle Dandy</u>, is, quite clearly, to expose and ridicule the restrictive morality of a walled-in community that is fearful of new ideas which place conviviality above conformity. As in Lawrence's "England, My England", a vital young person is driven from the community but by the wrong, unenlightened people and for the wrong reasons.

Chapter Two

From Ritual to Romance in <u>Within</u> <u>the</u> <u>Gates</u> and
<u>Cock-A-Doodle</u> <u>Dandy</u>

> The writer can use traditional myths and varying
> degrees of consciousness (with Joyce and Mann perhaps
> most fully conscious in our time), and he often does
> so with no premeditated intention, working from
> symbolic equivalents in his own conscious....Just as
> there are varying degrees of consciousness, so there
> are varying degrees of fruitfulness in these uses of
> traditional patterns, ranging from dishonest fakery
> at one extreme to some of the subtlest ironic and
> imaginative organizations in our poetry at the other.

> Stanley Edgar Hyman "The Ritual View of Myth
> and the Mythic"

Sean O'Casey simultaneously mimics and modifies some distinguishing dimensions of myth, both Christian and pre-Christian, in his
<u>Within</u> <u>the</u> <u>Gates</u> (1934), a modern morality set amidst the vanish-
ing greenness of a crowded London park, and in his <u>Cock-A-Doodle</u>
<u>Dandy</u> (1949), an Aristophanic allegory situated in a drought-
seared, fence-enclosed Irish garden. Indeed, O'Casey's mythopoeic
imagination achieves a marriage of myths in these two dramas as
Christian clerics collide with fertility figures, maypole dancing
challenges formal Christian worship, and ancient fertility
symbols like the silver shaft and the cock's crimson crest
contrast with the pious parishioners' cross and rosary beads.
O'Casey's basic intent, however, seems to be a desire to use myth
both structurally and satirically: (1) to employ myth as a means
of organizing his dramas into ritual sequences, and (2) to employ
myth as a satiric strategem which accentuates the difference
between the function of mythico-ritualistic elements in the lives
of ancient and modern man. Emphasizing the degenerative adapta-
tion of antique mythical patterns—patterns designed to restore
potency to people and provinces—O'Casey apparently laments
modern man's reluctance to enter joyously into the rites of
revivification which could redeem and revitalize both self and
society—the sick soul and the modern wasteland.

The sequence of events in both plays is similar. <u>Within</u> <u>the</u> <u>Gates</u>
records the progressive disintegration of a young London prosti-
tute named Jannice who has been abandoned by her father, the
Bishop; terrified by nuns, with their obsessive concern with sin
and the landscape of hell; reviled and shoved about by her
drunken mother, the Old Woman; and exploited and then discarded
by a motley of scheming males concerned primarily with sexual

17

gratification and social security. Unsuccessful in her attempts
to find enduring love and laughter, Jannice finally dies dancing
and the Dreamer, her friend and wandering minstrel, laments her
passing from the park which is congested with cynics, religious
extremists, and the shuffling Down-and-Outs. Cock-A-Doodle Dandy
likewise chronicles the career of a vital, young woman named
Loreleen who also wants a courageous, compassionate companion in
love with life. Instead, Loreleen is exploited and manhandled by
Sailor Mahan and other lusty males, denigrated and stoned by the
Irish villagers, and then reviled and sent into exile by Father
Domineer, a one-dimensional clerical villain who influences
virtually all aspects of life in Nyadnanave, Irish nest of
knaves. The other attractive and vital village women and Robin
Adair, another wandering minstrel,[1] follow Loreleen into exile,
leaving the cowardly and disconsolate villagers to fondle their
rosary beads--their clerical chains.

It is in the constantly evolving natural settings in both plays
that we first discover the birth-growth-decay pattern so promi-
nent in various vegetation and fertility[2] rituals designed to
mirror the fundamental rhythm of nature.[2] Cyclical in design,
O'Casey's dramas are clearly arranged in a ritualistic fashion so
as to serve as symbolic representations of the birth and death of
one year and one day.[3] The four scenes in Within the Gates, for
example, move us from the splendor of spring to the starkness of
winter. Scene I unfolds in the park on a clear spring morning as
birds search for food and build nests, fowl swim in the water or
preen themselves on the banks, and yellow daffodils reach for the
sun. A chorus of young boys and girls, representing trees and
flowers, enters to sing "Our Mother the Earth is a Maiden Again."
A sexual union is suggested as the Earth Maiden seeks out her
bridegroom, the Sun, in the "lovely confusion" of birds, blossoms, and buds. Scene II occurs during a summer noon yet the
colors are now chiefly golden glows tinged with gentle reds. The
daffodils have been replaced by hollyhocks with cluster beneath
the shrubbery. Red and yellow leaves flutter to the ground and
the sunflowers are "gaunt" in Scene III, set on an autumn
evening. It is a cold winter's night in Scene IV and the bare
branches of the trees form strange patterns against the black
canopy of the sky. Only the light from three stars penetrates the
chilly darkness.

A similar yet drastically abbreviated cyclical pattern is visible
in Cock-A-Doodle Dandy as we move from morning brilliance to
evening darkness. Scene I takes place in the garden in front of
bog owner Michael Marthraun's house on a glorious summer morning
as tough grass, buttercups, daisies, and sunflowers struggle to
retain their vivid vitality in the midst of a long drought that
has tinted the vegetation with a deep yellow hue. It is noon of
the same day in Scene II and although a strong breeze causes the

Irish Tricolor to stand out from its flagpole, the "sunshine isn't quite so bright and determined."[4] Scene III occurs appropriately at dusk of the same day now much colder. The vivid reds, greens, and yellows of the earlier scenes have now been replaced by sombre hues. As the sun sets, the flagpole and house stand black against the sky; the sunflowers have also turned a "solemn black" and the evening star is but faintly visible.

The discernible changes in the landscape are correlated with corresponding changes, both physical and psychological, which the two young women, Jannice and Loreleen, undergo as they interact with others, especially the two clergymen. In Scene I of Within the Gates, Jannice, despite her concern for her fainting spells resulting from a defective heart, is identified as a courageous and sensitive person whose main desire is "for a bright time of it." She affirms: "If I have to die, I'll die game; I'll die dancing!"[5] In Scene II Jannice is still hopeful and tenacious as she seeks the Bishop's support in arranging a marriage with Ned, the Gardener, and she assures the Dreamer that she has not forgotten his "sweet song" with its carpe diem thesis. Jannice is both faltering and frantic during the cold greyness of the autumn evening in Scene III. Often pale and short of breath, she is increasingly fearful of the fiery torment which she thinks she must endure because of her many transgressions. In the final bleak winter scene, Jannice, breathing erratically with a fixed look of fear on her face, must be supported by the Dreamer in the dancing which she attempts. Drained of energy, she finally collapses and dies as the Bishop assists her in making the sign of the cross.

A New Day Dawns

Yet O'Casey's young woman may not have danced and died in vain. Shortly after her demise the purple-black sky begins to change as it is pierced with golden shafts of light, "as if the sun was rising, and a new day about to begin."[6] Moreover, the Old Woman predicts: "A few more moments of time, and Spring'll be dancing among us again...the birds'll be busy at building small worlds of their own...the girls will go rambling round, each big with the thought of life in the loins of young men...."[7] The seasonal sequence prepares to repeat itself.

Loreleen's career follows an analogous course in Cock-A-Doodle Dandy. Amidst the dazzle of the summer morning in Scene I, Loreleen is jaunty and confident, blowing kisses and chiding the villagers for their rejection of revelry in favor of religion. In Scene II Loreleen—illuminated with golden shafts of light—dances, drinks toasts to the dancing cock, symbol of the élan

19

vital in man and nature, and defies the priest who fears the
lovely but shameless young women who tempt men to sin with their
indecent dress. With the coming of the chilly dusk of Scene III,
however, Loreleen loses her composure and her face reflects
"intense fright." Her clothes torn and disarranged, her face
bruised and bloody, she pleads with Father Domineer to show
mercy; he refuses. As Loreleen departs from the gloomy garden of
deepening darkness, the Messenger pleads for the gracious women
to come forth in "gold garments" or "reckless raiment" so that
the hopeful may "dance along through Ireland gay."[8] Unlike
Jannice, Loreleen may continue her quest and the Messenger's last
lyric hints that May Day rites will continue to occur despite the
unrelenting and harsh efforts of clerics like Father Domineer to
suppress or eradicate them: "Or lads follow lassies out nutting
in May/Forever and ever and ever!"[9]

As two women of beauty, passion, and vigorous affirmation,
Jannice and Loreleen emerge as fertility figures whose function
is to restore or release energies in both the withering waste-
lands and their infirm inhabitants--the dead souls. Moreover, the
names of both contain mythopoeic overtones. The name Jannice
links O'Casey's dancing protagonist with Janus, the Roman god of
doorways and the special patron of all new undertakings.[10] As god
of beginnings, Janus' blessing was sought at the beginning of
each day, month and year, and at all births, the beginning of
life. Jannice is, therefore, O'Casey's guardian of the park
gates, and is the fair maid alluded to in the May Day rites in
the early moments of Scene I as the chorus of young boys and
girls sing "Our Mother the Earth is a Maiden Again."

Like her Roman namesake, Jannice is also a woman with two faces
or two distinct aspects to her person. At intervals she thinks of
prayer, penance, and self-denial; at other times she favors wine,
song, dancing, and sexual self-indulgence. Anxious to emphasize
this dichotomy in his heroine, O'Casey thereby links Jannice with
Diana, another Roman goddess with two faces. Diana was, as most
myth students know, the guardian of flocks and fields, the chaste
goddess of the hunt. Hence hers was largely a migratory life of
abstinence. Yet Sir James Frazer points out in The Golden Bough
that Diana evolved from earlier, more primitive fertility figures
in ancient vegetation ceremonies. Thus Diana, "as goddess of
nature in general, and of fertility in particular," also came to
be regarded as "a personification of the teeming life of nature,
both animal and vegetable."[11] Hence Diana was associated with
both chastity and sensuality.

Although Diana was frequently depicted with a bow, quiver, and
javelin, she was also sometimes identified with a crescent. It is
not accidental, therefore, that O'Casey repeatedly stresses the
fact that his Jannice has a black crescent on her head and a

20

scarlet one on her hip. Jannice's mother, for example, mentions this detail twice in Scene IV, reminding us again of the psychic ambivalence of the heroine. Additionally, the Dreamer reinforces this woman-nature, fertility goddess motif in Scene II when he compares Jannice's legs to the fresh, golden branches of a willow, and her breasts to gay, white apple blossoms. Again in Scene II he states that Jannice's hand resembles a lovely, blue-veined, pink-tipped lily.

As a fertility figure, Jannice is pursued by many of the males in the park, but it is Ned the Gardener who celebrates her physical beauty in song. Moreover, it is the Gardener's singing that inspires the group of couples to sing of an earlier garden when Adam first saw Eve's "beauty shining through a mist of golden hair."[12] Additionally, it is the Gardener who carries the black maypole, ancient phallic symbol, that is to be used in the folk dancing designed to make England "merry again." Moreover, it is the Man with the Stick who lectures the Gardener about the maypole as "symbol" in Scene I, informing him that "It represents life, new life about to be born; fertility; th' urge wot was in the young lass (Jannice) you hunted away."[13] It is appropriate, therefore, for the chorus of young girls and boys dancing around the maypole to sing the folk song "Haste to the Wedding" because Jannice repeatedly insists that she must have a husband, child, and home to be fulfilled. Ironically, the Gardener does not really want to make things grow; he shuns marriage and so must carry a black maypole, symbolic of his denial of life's creative urges.

Loreleen's name likewise evokes myth. Like the Lorelei of German legend, she is given the alluring traits of a temptress who would lure men to their ruin. In Scene III Father Domineer associates her with the snake and the Garden of Eden. Both Father Domineer and bog owner Marthraun agree that it is the "soft stimulatin' touch" of woman's flesh and the graceful, provocative movements of "good-lookin' women" like Loreleen which place men in peril. Yet Loreleen would tempt men to live not die--would tempt men and women to reject domestic drudgery and Christian duty for dalliance and dance. As defender-performer of the Dionysian dance, Loreleen is likened to a "flower" that has been blown by a winsome wind into a "dread, dried-up desert."[14] Because she is responsive to the fundamental rhythms of life, especially sexual and instinctive, she is consistently identified with the color green. When she arrives from London in Scene I she wears a dark green dress and a "saucy" hat of brighter green; when she departs in Scene III, refusing to be suffocated under Father Domineer's black clerical cape, she wears a green cloak over her shoulders, an external sign of her inner vitality. Moreover, Loreleen, like Jannice, is associated with the color scarlet--a color which hints at both passion and piety--voluptuous woman and fallen

21

woman--in both plays. If Jannice has a scarlet crescent on her
hip, Loreleen has a scarlet crescent on her hat, an ornament
which resembles a cock's crimson crest, and it is the crowing
cock, with his vivid colors and agile movements, who is obviously
an incarnation of the eros of life that animates both men and
nature in Cock-A-Doodle Dandy.

Two Priests as Fisher Kings

If the two questers resemble fertility figures, the two clerics
remind us of the sick fisher king whose illness brings a blight--
a plague--to the land. The Bishop in Within the Gates, a man of
sixty, has lost much of his vitality, and O'Casey indicates that
his powers are "beginning to fail."[15] Comfortable, complacent,
and hypocritical, he refuses to involve himself in the sordid
stress and strife of daily life; he peddles pious platitudes in
the religious debates; ignores the murder, rape, suicide, and
divorce headlines in the daily press; pats babies of respectable
parents on the head; refuses alms to the poor; and recoils from
many of the pleas of Jannice, his daughter sired when he was a
young theology student. With his concern for ritual and social
decorum, his aloofness and his general ineptness, the Bishop has
helped create the despairing cynicism, atheism, and amoral
opportunism--the spiritual plague--which affects the lives of the
Down-and-Out, the men with hats, the chair attendants, the
nursemaids, and others in the park-wasteland. His encounters with
Jannice, however, help him discover his deficiencies, and he
manifests new energy, humility, and compassionate purpose in his
actions at the play's close. Jannice has assisted at his rebirth,
which bodes well for future park visitors.

Such is not the case with Father Domineer in Cock-A-Doodle Dandy.
An inflexible father who would frighten people into obedience,
Domineer defends tradition against individual talent while raging
at the carnal desires of men.[16] A bigot and a bully, he has a
restricted and restrictive religious code distinguished by an
abnormal, Jansenistic fear of the flesh. He surrounds himself
with unthinking sycophants who assist him in his activities which
include physical abuse, exorcisms, ceremonial marches, and
caustic, non-Christian tirades. Loreleen cannot enlighten and
liberate this cleric, and so the spiritual desolation must remain
to stifle the conforming souls of Nyadnanave. The clerical chains
remain to choke or confine those who lack the courage to rebel
and depart like the young woman in green.

If the two clergymen remind us of the fisher king and his drought
or pestilence-plagued land of pre-Christian myth, the two young

22

men who perform choral functions in the two dramas—the Dreamer in Within the Gates and the Messenger in Cock-A-Doodle Dandy— resemble the wandering minstrels of earlier historical interludes. With his soft, broad-rimmed hat and vivid orange scarf, the Dreamer lives off the land, wandering from place to place to peddle his poetry. He gives money to Jannice from the advance which he has received on a book that is to be published, and he patiently strives to diminish Jannice's fear of hellish punishment. After Jannice's death he asserts that God will find room for one "scarlet Blossom" among his "thousand white lillies," and he hopes that future children will "sing and laugh and play where these have moaned in misery."[17] The Messenger wears a silvery-grey coat adorned with a pair of scarlet wings, green beret and sandals, carries a silver staff, and leads the strutting cock around with a green ribbon.[18] Hence he resembles the messenger—attendant to the gods of Greek and Roman myth. Yet his name Robin Adair links him with the Robin Hood romances. With his accordian and gentle airs, this Ariel-like figure finally departs with maid Marion, affirming that passionate young men and women will always obey the impulse to circumvent clerics to engage in the ancient and exhilarating fertility rites of spring.

It is apparent, therefore, that O'Casey both contrasts and commingles ancient ritual and modern, ironic romance in these two ceremonial, song-seasoned dramas, utilizing a congeries of provocative mythical constructs to impose design upon his material and to accentuate his satiric indictment of modern man's spiritual decline. O'Casey admitted that in writing Within the Gates he had attempted to "bring back to drama the music and song and dance of the Elizabethan play and the austere ritual of Greek drama, caught up and blended with life around us."[19] Later he adds: "Within the Gates. Probably could be, maybe is, a 'Morality Play,' tho' I didn't write it from that viewpoint. I had myth in mind."[20]

As for Cock-A-Doodle Dandy O'Casey apparently wanted observers to view Loreleen's career as a duplication, with variations, of ancient scapegoat ceremonials. According to Frazer, the scapegoat pattern involved a three-part process: first, a sin-saturated community (like Nyadnanave) isolated one talented, handsome, or possessed individual as its leader or representative; this community then paid extravagant homage to this hero-scapegoat for a time; finally the community exiled or killed its hero. The sins and guilt feelings of the community, concentrated in the victim-hero, were expiated by his departure or death, and so the community, with men like Marthraun walking its streets, is free to live in relative peace until the cyclical pattern demands another "crucifixion" for community cleansing. Laureen's career embraces all the major features outlined by Frazer in a manner that is, to be sure, more than coincidental.[21]

23

Certainly the ritual—the patterned pageantry of the past—is
transparently present in both of these plays, but the romance is
not. True, lovely maidens, wearing gay garments and rehearsing
high hopes, dance spiritedly but all too briefly through a green,
pastoral world, but the handsome, knightly male, with his height-
ened ethical awareness and love of comradeship and challenge, is
largely absent, replaced by sycophants, false seers, and gombeen
men. And it is the mythical patterns which become the objective
correlatives in these ritual-romance dramas, facilitating the
audiences' cognition of O'Casey's bias for an age with a greater
fondness for and commitment to faith and frolic than our own.

CHAPTER THREE

PRELUDE

The Decline of Families and Traditions

In his volume of verse The Winding Stair (1933) William Butler
Yeats places "Coole Park and Ballylee, 1931", a poem that reflects his persistent awareness of history as a "darkening flood"
that erodes and washes away marriages, alliances and families.
Remembering his relationship with Lady Augusta Gregory, the
strong-minded and courageous woman involved in the Irish literary
renaissance, Yeats describes the beauty of Coole Park--its
orderly house and terraced grounds ("ancestral trees" and "gardens rich in memory")--and he associates Lady Gregory with the
continuity of a tradition in Ireland that cherished courtesy, the
arts and ceremony. This particular family line was to end with
the death of the last inheritor (Major Robert Gregory) in World
War I. As Yeats explains:

>   We were the last romantics--choose for theme
>   Traditional sanctity and loveliness;
>   Whatever's written in what poets name
>   The book of the people; whatever most can bless
>   The mind of man or elevate a rhyme;
>   But all is changed, that high horse riderless,
>   Though mounted in that saddle Homer rode
>   Where the swan drifts upon a darkening flood.[1]

The high, riderless horse menaced by the "darkening flood"
emphasizes Yeats' persistent fear of the disruption and displace-
ment of the aristocratic Anglo-Irish tradition, with its great
houses and ceremonial existence, by a reckless horde of active
nationalists. Earlier in "Meditations in Time of Civil War"
(1928), Yeats had fretted about his own physical weakness and
indecision amidst the tragic destruction of these great houses in
Ireland by roving bands of soldiers. Reacting with dismay and
despair at the loss of these old monuments, Yeats acknowledges
that these great country houses were built by rich and aggressive
men of power, by men who would use others to achieve their grand
design. Yet Yeats also sadly observes that this aggressiveness--
this will to action--is largely lacking in the descendants of
these earlier builders.

Turning then to himself as a defender of this eroding tradition
and to his tower-home at Thoor Ballylee (a lesser, surrogate great
house), Yeats wonders about the previous owner of the tower, a
man-of-arms who seemed to be a historical castaway, a man left in

loneliness after endless "night alarms" and "long wars." Regarding himself as another historical castaway engulfed by the dark flood of history, Yeats broods about what he will leave to his "bodily heirs", a thought that leads into a joyful, meditative interlude about how customs and finely fashioned artifacts are preserved and transmitted by certain families down through the centuries. Reminding himself that his heirs must content themselves with the "emblems of adversity" which he will leave behind in his tower (certainly his art which hopefully will survive), Yeats worries about how his children will manage in future years when bees build hives in the crevices of the loosening masonry of his tower and when the regulating patterns of a stable society have been erased by an angry mob dancing to a frenzied drum or clamorous gong.

Yeats' concern with the disappearance of the Anglo-Irish tradition reappears in Purgatory (1939), a historical allegory that again underscores his passionate regret for the collapse of the old order in Ireland. As in Words on the Window-Pane, the spirits of the dead return to reenact certain passionate moments in their lives, and these dead have a jolting impact upon the living in this late play. Like the departed mother in James Joyce's "The Dead", the dead mother in Purgatory agitates her son, her brief visit serving to remind the thoughtful son of what once was—of a vanished time of stability, family wealth, and hope now beyond reclamation. Yet Yeats emphasizes the self-destructive, consuming fires of lust in the dead mother in Purgatory, a woman whose overwhelming passions caused her to surrender to the rough hands of a stable hand.

Telescoping time and interlocking quickly the various levels of meaning in his allegory, Yeats despairs over the future of Ireland (and other nations as well) as suspicion, greed, lust, and hatred determine much of modern man's conduct. So as in "Among School Children", Yeats looks closely at the "dying generations", with each successive generation lacking some of those qualities—control, compassion, assertiveness, and awareness of noblesse oblige—which their forefathers possessed. Tragically lamenting the loss of all that which was enlightened and ceremonious in previous times, Yeats recoils from the new man, a Swiftian, half-witted Yahoo who must be stabbed to death by his father to prevent additional pollution of the family and race. Selecting details which are both authoritative and evocative, Yeats creates, then, a powerful drama of stark simplicity and complex texture, a drama-as-history lesson about the breakup of the Anglo-Irish heritage in Yeats' native land.

Samuel Beckett also studies the fragmentation of a family and the problems that come with the passage of time—problems like the bothersome decline of physical vigor and beauty with the

attendant melancholy awareness of missed opportunities--in
Krapp's Last Tape (1958), a monodrama about a miserly old man, a
human grotesque, who drinks booze, stuffs banana peelings into
his pockets, listens to tapes, and waits for Miss McGlome,
another exile from Connaught, Ireland, to sing her evening songs.
Like Yeats' Old Man, Beckett's Krapp is also very entangled in
his memories of the past (many of them recorded on his tapes)
which involve the life and death of his mother, his separation
from a young woman with incomparable, chrysolite eyes, and his
unsuccessful literary efforts. Less of a parable about history
than Yeats' work, Krapp's Last Tape stresses the painful isolation that must come to a man who was too miserly to share himself
and his possessions with others. Unwilling to involve himself
with a woman in any extended relationship, Krapp sires no sons or
daughters to continue the family line. An inhibited, increasingly
neurotic observer of life, Krapp has become, therefore, the
shriveled, hard, black ball which his name connotes, an old man
condemned to wander in the stagnant gloom of his cluttered den, a
constipated old man both sustained and tormented by his memories
of better days.

Chapter Three

Yeats and Beckett: Old Men and Memories:

> Sometimes a spirit re-lives not the pain of death
> but some passionate or tragic moment of life.
> Swedenborg describes this and gives the reason for
> it. There is an incident of this kind in the
> Odyssey, and many in Eastern literature; the
> murderer repeats his murder, the robber his robbery,
> the lover his serenade, the soldier hears the
> trumpets once again. If I were a Catholic I would
> say that such spirits were in Purgatory. In vain we
> do write requiescat in pace upon the tomb, for they
> must suffer, and we in turn must suffer until God
> gives peace.

Yeats, The Words Upon the Window-Pane

Two old men do relive some passionate and tragic moments of their
disappointing, futile lives in William Butler Yeats' Purgatory, a
concentrated one act tragedy first visualized as a scene of
"tragic intensity" which focuses on a despairing pedlar and two
acts of parricide in a family tragedy which demonstrates the
demoralizing return of the past, and Samuel Beckett's Krapp's
Last Tape, a one act monodrama focusing upon a shabby old man
sipping drinks and rummaging among cardboard boxes for some
recorded tapes that will momentarily recreate his past for him.
"Dreaming back," both old men re-experience some joyful and
painful but similar experiences from their pasts: their days of
youthful vigor when the world was alive with color, movement, and
hope; their different involvements in the deaths of their
fathers; their ambivalent reactions to the decline and deaths of
their mothers, one of whom marries a stable hand; their romantic
and lustful affairs with younger women, one a beauty and the
other a tramp; and the inexorable erosion of their early dreams
and ambitions that were replaced by despair and cynical, obscene
jesting with the passage of the years. "Drowned in dreams," the
two old men inhabit a purgatory where emotions are recollected in
a despairing and anxiety-ridden tranquility, a tranquility that
threatens to verge off into hysterical defiance and rage or
hopeless submission.

Perhaps a summary of the action in Yeats' stark but endlessly
suggestive Purgatory--his last dramatic work involving ghosts who
do not speak--might be the most useful way of initiating this
investigation of these two remarkable but different plays about
old men manipulated by their memories. In this play an old
pedlar and his bastard son arrive at the ruins of a country
house that stands before a bare tree and that once belonged to the

28

old pedlar's mother, a lady of some affluence and social standing who, nevertheless, could not always control her passions. In an impulsive but fateful moment of lustful desire, she married a drunken groom who wasted her wealth on cards, horses, drink, and women. After his mother dies in giving birth to him--an event foreshadowed by an interlude of drunken sexual revelry with her base husband--the pedlar, now sixteen years of age, stabs his groom-father to death in the fire that destroys the great house:

> I stuck him with a knife,
> That knife that cuts my dinner now,
> And after that I left him in the fire.
> They dragged him out, somebody saw
> The knife-wound but could not be certain
> Because the body was all black and charred.
> Then some that were his drunken friends
> Swore they would put me upon trial,
> Spoke of quarrels, a threat I had made.
> The gamekeeper gave me some old clothes,
> I ran away, worked here and there
> Till I became a pedlar on the roads,
> No good trade, but good enough
> Because I am my father's son.
> Because of what I did or may do.[2]

Now it is the anniversary of the mother's wedding night and her shade, "dreaming back" in purgatory, must reenact the drunken sexual action in which the pedlar was begotten--a reenactment that enables the mother to experience both sexual delight and personal humiliation. Condemned to wander in misery in a purgatory of tormented souls, the mother cannot escape the consequences of her lustful, demeaning action; compulsively she must return to the "thought" that her submission to her drunken husband was the catalyst in a chain reaction that produced a flawed child, a human hybrid rent by the antithetical legacies in his person. Her son, the pedlar, has in turn sired a "bastard" son upon a tinker's daughter in a ditch, the continuation of the decline of the once unified family. This son reveals his basic greedy self when--his father distracted by the figure of his returned mother in the lighted window--he tries to steal the old man's bag of gold. Desperately anxious to halt this tragic decline and to release his mother's spirit from the purgatorial role assigned her, the pedlar stabs his bastard son to death as he recoils--in fear and amazement--from the two figures behind the lighted window in the ruined house, the pedlar using the same old jackknife he had used to slay his father many years earlier:

> That beast there would know nothing, being nothing.
> If I should kill a man under the window
> He would not even turn his head.   (He stabs the boy.)

29

My father and my son on the same jack-knife.
That finishes--there--there--there--
        (He stabs again and again. The window grows dark.)[3]

Then the apparitions vanish and the bare tree puts out a leaf,
but, moments later, the bridegroom's phantom horse is heard
again, and the cycle prepares to repeat itself. Overwhelmed with
despair, the pedlar then realizes that his double murder has not
released his mother from her torment:

> Twice a murderer and all for nothing,
> And she must animate that dead night
> Not once but many times!
>   O God,
> Release my mother's soul from its dream!
> Mankind can do no more. Appease
> The misery of the living and the remorse of the dead.[4]

Yeats' objectives in writing Purgatory were undoubtedly multiple,
but he clearly intended to give us--in the figure of the Old Man
pedlar--the anatomy of a divided soul, a soul reflecting the
conflicting legacies left it by the high-born but impulsive
mother and the coarse, hard-drinking father. Observing that the
Old Man's hybrid nature is reflected in his speech--sometimes
brutal and sometimes lyrical--Leonard E. Nathan writes:

> The Boy's thievery and half-threat to murder his
> father complete his character, as his father's
> character is completed by the ruthless killing of
> his son, an act which paradoxically reveals some-
> thing fine in the Old Man's nature, because this
> last murder was motivated by a wish to end his
> mother's terrible suffering. The Old Man's
> brutalized fineness is the only direct expression in
> the play of the lineal aristocratic superiority
> thrown away by his mother.[5]

Yet Yeats apparently had a larger objective in mind in devising
Purgatory, and this was his desire to fashion a play as political
parable, a parable that would trace and evaluate the drastic
political-economic changes in an Ireland that had gone from
eighteenth century restraint and elegance to twentieth century
exuberance and crassness. Central to this concern which gives
Yeats' play the additional dimensions of political allegory is
the ruined house, the major symbol in the play. As Donald R.
Pearce so rightly observes:

> Few symbols could better indicate the character and
> fate of the Anglo-Irish aristocratic tradition, as
> Yeats had come to view that tradition and its fate,

than a great house burned down by its drunken,
good-for-nothing master. To Yeats that tradition--
which, like the house in the play, goes back to
'Aughrim and the Boyne' and reached its peak in the
eighteenth century--was the one great political,
social and intellectual achievement of (modern)
Ireland.[6]

Thus the Old Man's references to the ruined house are central to
the play's larger implications. In his first speech to his
bastard son--a near witless lout who can but dimly perceive the
meaning in his father's disjointed catechism--the Old Man advises
his son to "Study that house." He later adds that for a drunken
gamekeeper to destroy such a house so that its threshold could be
used to patch a pig sty is a "capital offense":

> Great people lived and died in this house:
> Magistrates, colonels, members of Parliament,
> Captains and Governors, and long ago
> Men that had fought at Aughrim and the Boyne,
> Some that had gone on Government work
> To London or to India came home to die,
> Or came from London every spring
> To look at the May-blossoms in the park.
> They had loved the trees that he cut down
> To pay what he had lost at cards
> Or spent on the horses, drink and women;
> Had loved the house, had loved all
> The intricate passages of the house,
> But he killed the house; to kill a house
> where great men grew up, married, died,
> I hear declare a capital offence.[7]

Yeats Blames the Indulgent Rich

Yet the indulgent aristocracy were partially responsible--so
Yeats suggests--for their own ruin because the willingness of the
Old Man's mother to marry the groom beneath her was the initial
act that made possible the tragedy. As Pearce argues: "The
marriage between the high born mother and the training-stable
groom expresses for Yeats the debasement of the aristocratic
tradition (In Ireland in particular, in Europe in general) by
degenerate alliances."[8] Hence the date of the play's composition
and the references to the number sixteen are vital to the play's
political implications. As Pearce again explains:

> Yeats emphasizes....that the young boy is sixteen
> years old; calculating from the time the play was
> written (1938) the boy was born, therefore, in 1922,

31

the year of the founding of the Irish Free State.
[Hence] The offspring of this marriage (latter-day
nationalism) slew the father--(degenerate landlord-
ism), took to the roads as a pedlar (of popular
materialistic nationalism throughout the country)
and, in the old man's words, 'got upon a tinker's
daughter in a ditch' (proletarian Ireland) a bastard
son (the Modern Free State) who has neither memory
of, nor belief in, the old man's tale.[9]

If the Old Man first advises his son to "Study that house," he
later advises the audience to "Study that tree," the second major
symbolical property in the play which acquires different meanings
in different contexts. Early in the play when the Old Man asks
his son what the tree is like, the boy answers: "A silly old
man."[10] A bare thing "riven" by a thunderbolt, the tree is an
appropriate symbol for the old man--also time-worn--who leads a
nomadic, relatively barren life despite the presence of his
coarse companion, his son. Remembering fifty years ago when the
house was intact and the tree alive, the Old Man next associates
the then flourishing tree with leaves "thick as butter" and with
"fat, greasy life," epithets intended to evoke the orgiastic
delight which the Old Man's mother, "mad" with desire for her
half-drunk husband with whiskey bottle under his arm, experienced
when she led her new, animalistic mate to her chamber on their
wedding night. Finally, in the third reference to the tree
following the stabbing of his son, the Old Man completes his
catechism by counseling:

                    Study that tree.
          It stands there like a purified soul,
          All cold, sweet, glistening light.
          Dear mother, the window is dark again,
          But you are in the light because
          I finished all that consequence.
          I killed that lad because had he grown up
          He would have struck a woman's fancy,
          Begot, and passed pollution on.
          I am a wretched foul old man
          And therefore harmless. When I have stuck
          This old jack-knife into a sod
          And pulled it out bright again,
          And picked up all the money that he dropped,
          I'll to a distant place, and there
          Tell my old jokes among new men.[11]

Convinced that he has finished the "consequences" of his mother's
rash action, the Old Man is quickly disappointed and so the tree
is--in his imagination--but a "purified soul" for all too brief a
time. Isolating Purgatory as a play deviating from the No play

patterns so pronounced in Yeats' earlier works, Nathan cites
Yeats' fondness for the "binding metaphor" that gives cohesion to
his play:

> The fruitless, stricken tree, which the boy rightly
> associates with the old age of manhood, is also an
> emblem of the ruined house that was once rich and of
> the family that was once healthy and fruitful. The
> nature of the play's action links tree, house, and
> familial line in the wider implication of a general
> bastardization, coarsening, and decay of life.
> Moreover, the tree is not only a natural symbol for
> the last stage in a cycle of birth, growth, and
> decay; this particular tree is ruined, riven by a
> thunderbolt, and will not blossom again....The tree
> is now identified with his mother's spirit, purged
> both of 'fat, greasy' human life and of that life's
> corruption and ruin.[12]

Hence _Purgatory_ is Yeats' complex drama of natural-
supernaturalism, a probing character study of an old man moti-
vated to kill twice because of his lingering respect for a
vanished, admirable past and his abiding love for his dead but
tormented mother, and a symbolic dramatic chronicle of the
historical forces which Yeats saw disrupting and transforming his
native land. In this historical process the members of the
Anglo-Irish tradition, like some of the members of the pre-Civil
War South in William Faulkner's fiction, are depicted as victims
fated for extinction in the process of natural selection enabling
the previously submerged lower classes to rise to positions of
power and relative affluence. Tragically, these people of the
vanishing aristocracy lacked the moral courage and the physical
stamina to compete with the new, assertive members of successive
generations, generations increasingly mean and mercenary. Reminding one of the pathetic and apathetic landed gentry in Chekhov's
The Cherry Orchard, Yeats' survivors from an earlier, more
cultivated time were too indulgent and complacent, and too little
involved, as enlightened citizens, in Ireland's protean political
tumult. The tragic result was the emergence of a new age in which
"The best lack all conviction, while the worst are full of
passionate intensity."[13]

Written in 1958, nineteen years after Yeats' _Purgatory_,
Samuel Beckett's _Krapp's Last Tape_ is not a verse play about the
decline of a tradition, but it is another amazingly complex,
one-act play about the fragmentation of a family (both the father
and mother die as in Yeats' play) and, more precisely, about the
intense and complex emotional involvement (an attachment fueled
in part, by hatred) which a brooding son has with his mother.
This son, Krapp, rejects his opportunities for human involvement
and, like Mr. Duffy in James Joyce's "A Painful Case", retreats

33

into his residence, a dark "den" cluttered with his personal belongings. He does, however, venture out of his den in one moment of personal crisis to maintain a death watch for his mother (he wishes that she were dead), a major episode in this memory play which, like Yeats' Purgatory, repays careful analysis.

The opening movement of Beckett's play, an extended pantomime recalling the familiar, puzzling antics of the circus clown or the sad-faced comedian from silent films, flashes forth a cluster of clues about Krapp's character, directs our attention to objects (the bananas, the bunch of keys, locked desk and envelope) which steadily accrue greater symbolic valency, and establishes the contrast of colors (black versus white) that subsequently mirrors Krapp's painful, unresolved duality. This pantomime is played out in Krapp's den, a den being the lair of a wild animal, a hollow or cavern used as a hideout, a center for secret activity, or a small, usually squalid, secluded dwelling. Krapp is, indeed, animal-man in self-imposed hibernation, a "wearish old man" who has a "purple nose", a "cracked voice", a "laborious walk" and who is near-sighted and hard of hearing. A miserly, compulsive Collector Man who prefers his old rags to clean, properly fitting clothes, Krapp wears rusty black trousers too short for him and a rusty black, sleeveless waistcoat with four capacious pockets, the pockets serving as his personal filing cabinets where he stashes keys, an envelope and a partially-eaten banana. Krapp has also collected the tapes that summarize the major events in his long, unfulfilled life, and these have been stored in cardboard boxes which rest on his table with the two drawers which is situated front center in bright, white light with the table's two drawers facing the audience. The rest of the den is in darkness.

Addicted to Bananas and Booze

Krapp's first actions as he sits at the table facing front is to heave a great sigh and to look at his "heavy" watch at the end of a chain, the despairing actions of a man tired of living and weary of dragging his watch and chain around as if they were a ball and chain. After examining the envelope, Krapp moves around to the front of the table and, after unlocking and relocking the first drawer, unlocks and takes a large banana from the second drawer. He then advances to the edge of the stage where he halts, strokes the banana, peels it, drops the skin at his feet, and puts the end of the banana in his mouth. After staring "vacuously" at the audience, he bites off the end of the banana, and then begins to pace to and fro at the edge of the stage, "meditatively" eating the banana. When he subsequently trips on the skin and almost falls, he pushes the peeling off the stage with his foot. He then duplicates this desk-heavy sigh-key-banana sequence, omitting only the glance at the heavy watch. This

opening, silent prelude ends when Krapp, excited by a sudden
idea, charges "with all the speed he can muster", into the
backstage darkness where, after a ten-second delay, he pops a
cork and has his first drink of the evening. Krapp will retreat
into this darkness at later intervals for additional refreshment,
drinks that cause him to break into song and to walk unsteadily,
and yet he maintains the ten-second delay between all his drinks.
Thus he does make a sustained effort to control his desire for
drink, one aspect of his life-long struggle to discipline his
appetites.

While offering some oblique, initial glimpses into Krapp's self-
indulgent, hedonistic tendencies (the two symbolic bananas
suggesting a fondness, perhaps an addiction, to oral gratification and masturbation), this opening segment certainly raises a
number of questions: Why has Krapp retreated into this dark den
whose only illumination is the "strong white light" above his
cluttered table? Why has he kept the envelope? Why does he lock
his bananas in the drawer of the table and then seat himself at
the table across from the locked drawer? Why does he keep his
drink some distance from his desk, an inconvenient arrangement
that forces him to exert himself with rapid movements when thirst
motivates him and to fumble in the dark for his drink? Subsequent
segments of the play provide answers to these important questions.

When Krapp returns, after a fifteen-second delay, from the
backstage darkness, he is carrying an old ledger which he is
anxious to open; he betrays his impatience by placing the ledger
on the table and then rubbing his hands together in anticipation.
When he exclaims "Ah!", his first utterance in the play, sound is
added to setting and movement. Turning the pages, he halts at the
entry, box three, spool five. With relish, he repeats "spool" and
then "spooool", adding two o's to the word so as to extend it and
to prolong his pleasure in reciting it, a speech pattern that
remains unchanged and reappears at later intervals in the play.
Why "spooool" should bring a "Happy Smile" to Krapp's old face
puzzles the audience at this early juncture in the play. Viewers
later discover that "spooool" is part of the associational
movement of Krapp's active mind, a mind fond of a pun that
extracts stool from "spooool". Thus "spooool" triggers a quick
mental sequence that associates the spools of precious tape with
stools, the pleasurable shits which Krapp longs to experience but
can't because of his chronic constipation.

After carefully extracting spool five from box three and placing
it on the machine, Krapp, again rubbing his hands together in
anticipatory delight, reads aloud the ledger entry which identifies the major episodes on the tape. A table of contents listing
the six major concerns during an emotional, transitional year in
Krapp's life, this ledger entry includes references to the death

35

of Krapp's mother, the black ball, the dark nurse, Krapp's bowel condition, Memorable Equinox, and a farewell to love. When the brooding Krapp subsequently assumes a listening posture, leaning forward with elbows on the table and one hand cupping one ear towards the machine, the audience does likewise. A brief delay follows when Krapp, furious at knocking one of the boxes off the table, "violently" sweeps all the boxes and ledger to the floor. Again we discover that Krapp's attempts at self-control—at mastering his passions—are often unsuccessful.

The audience is subsequently jolted when a strong voice, identified by Beckett as Krapp's at a much earlier time, explodes from the tape, a pompous voice asserting that, on his thirty-ninth birthday, Krapp is, except for his "old weakness" of constipation, "sound as a bell" and near the "crest" of his intellectual powers. This second voice will speak most of the lines in the vocal duet that follows, a duet serving as the extended, explanatory middle of the play which asks that the audience accompany old Krapp on his time-tripping journey back into his vanished past.

The taped voice subsequently introduces us to Krapp-at-39 who is not that different from the older Krapp whom we have already met. An "isolato" already at thirty-nine, Krapp had celebrated by himself his birthday, an "awful occasion", at a deserted wine-house where he sat with closed eyes before the fire, sorting out the tangled skeins of his life. He had observed several earlier birthdays in a similar fashion. After separating "the grain from the husks", he jotted down his conclusions on the back of an envelope, presumably the same envelope which the elder Krapp now carries about in his waistcoat pocket. Krapp-at-39 later explains that "grain" represents "those things worth having" when all his dust is settled. Yet the younger Krapp adds that it was "good" to leave the winehouse to return to his den and his "old rags." He is, however, troubled because he has gorged himself with three bananas (he could barely restrain himself from devouring a fourth), "fatal things" for a man with his chronic constipation. He also acknowledges that the new light above his table is a "great improvement", inducing him to feel "less alone" in the surrounding darkness. In the "extraordinary silence" of the evening, he wonders if old Miss McGlome, that wonderful, old woman from Connaught, Ireland, will sing the songs of her girlhood, a thought which forces Krapp to admit that he was never, as a boy and a man, a singer.

The pause which follows is a transitional signal that prepares Krapp-at-39 and the audience for another time-tripping sequence, a journey back of 10-12 years to Kedar Street when Krapp, then 29 or 31, was living with Bianca with the "incomparable" eyes in a relationship which is described as a "hopeless business."

Admitting that he has been listening to random passages from this "old year", Krapp finds it difficult to believe that he was ever that "young whelp" with all those "aspirations" and "resolutions". Significantly, the aspirations—and the temptations—of Krapp-at-29 are the very same ones that later torment Krapp-at-39 and the older Krapp: to drink less, to have a "less engrossing sexual life", to strive for "unattainable laxation", and to complete his "opus magnum". Krapp-at-29 also mentions the last illness of his father, a prelude to Krapp-at-39's reference to the death of his mother and one of the many parallel patterns in the play. Krapp-at-39's summary of Krapp-at-29's tape, presumably also made on his birthday, also includes the younger Krapp's references to his "flagging" pursuit of happiness and to his "yelp to Providence" which end Krapp-at-29's tape, details that cause the two elder Krapps to join together in a duet of cynical laughter. Krapp-at-39 finally concedes that all that remains of all that "earlier misery" is the memory of a girl in a shabby, green coat left behind at a railway station.

Disturbed by the talking memories of his past, Krapp switches off the machine and retreats into the backstage darkness where he attempts to diminish his mental anguish by downing three drinks, each drink separated, as with the previous one drink, by ten-second intervals. Yet the drink affects him and he responds with a "brief burst of quavering song"—a portion of the Evensong remembered from a vespers service in the Anglican communion which he attended earlier when he was in short trousers. Momentarily revitalized by the drink, Krapp returns to switch on the machine and to resume his listening posture, preparation that prepares for Krapp-at-39's complex reaction to the death of his mother, a traumatic event that jolted him, forcing him to see himself in a new light, to accept his—and everyone else's—mortality, and to engage in his last act of giving and sharing, an action involving a black ball and a white dog.

Krapp as Weaver-Bird

This significant segment, which assembles and accents in a concentrated cluster the critical events in Krapp's year of decision, a year in which he exerted himself to cut the cord linking him to his mother and one in which he rejected the companionship of another woman (his farewell to love), begins by mentioning the place where his mother lay "a-dying" in the late autumn after her long "viduity", the last word prompting Krapp to switch off the tape and to carry an "enormous dictionary" from the backstage darkness to his table to discover the word's meaning. The first definition—"condition of being a widow"— refers, of course, to his mother, but the second one, referring to the "vidua-bird" as an animal (a weaver-bird [male] with black plumage) surprises and delights the elderly Krapp because it presents him with an apt image of himself. Like the black-plumaged vidua-bird bringing sticks, straws and food to its nest, Krapp has constructed his own secluded, dark nest with boxes, tapes, banana skins and old rags.

Closing the dictionary, Krapp resumes listening to the tape which describes in detail Krapp's death watch. He is seated on a bench by a weir in the biting wind of autumn in a public area, a small park perhaps, with a small population of regulars, nursemaids, infants, old men and dogs, intently observing the window of the room in the building where his mother is living out her last moments. One dark, young beauty in a starched white uniform with an "incomparable" bosom and "chrysolite" eyes distracts Krapp during his death vigil by pushing a big, black hooded perambulator, "a most funeral thing", past him. An effective symbol appropriate for this setting, this perambulator joins both life and death: the infant in the carriage protected by the nursemaid will grow old all too quickly and will be ultimately transported to its funeral and its grave in a black hearse. Life is all too quickly followed by death--so flows the thought process of the brooding, shivering Krapp.

Then the dirty, brown blind in his mother's room goes down (the blind's movement suggesting the closing of the eyelids over the eyes of the recent dead) at precisely the same moment that Krapp is throwing a small ball to amuse a little white dog. Retrieving the ball, Krapp sits in meditative silence until he associates the ball with moments of time--his mother's moments, his moments, and the dog's moments. His subsequent description of the ball as a "small, old, black, hard, solid" object is simultaneously an apt description of himself, a miserly, aged Collector Man. When Krapp then confesses that he gave the ball to the dog, who took it "gently" in his mouth, he adds: "I might have kept it."[14] This seemingly casual disclosure is of critical importance because it suggests that Krapp's unexpected act of giving occurred only moments after his mother's death. Mysteriously, his mother's death had freed him momentarily from his selfish, grasping habits of a lifetime, and he responded in a surprising and uncharacteristic manner: he gave one of his possessions away. However, the rest of the drama suggests consistently that Krapp saved everything belonging to him after this one moment of unexpected generosity, even hoarding, as he later tells Fanny, his sperm.

In her massive and detailed Samuel Beckett: A Biography, Deirdre Bair discusses at length the autobiographical content in Krapp's Last Tape, and she mentions repeatedly the fierce, exhausting, and ambivalent struggle that Beckett had with his strong-willed mother, a struggle that lasted up until May Beckett's death in the summer of 1950 and a desperate battle that often drove

Beckett to his bed for days with cysts, boils, colds and aching
joints. Fascinated by Beckett's recurrent nightmarish intervals
of terror which left him constipated, drenched with sweat, and
overcome with a blind panic that threatened to suffocate him,
physician Geoffrey Thompson argued that Beckett's "eruptions"
were psychosomatic and were traceable to the "torrents of anger
and venom" he directed towards his mother.[15] Significantly, after
May Beckett's death, Beckett refused to accept any of his
mother's belongings. As Bair comments: "With this rejection of
May's effects, he had finally, symbolically, managed to kill
her."[16] Some such feeling of breaking free from his mother's
influence also affects Krapp in the death vigil by the weir, a
liberating experience that compels him to share, even perhaps
against his will, his possession (a black ball) with some other
living creature, the small white dog. This is Krapp's one visible
act of sharing in the play.

Predictably, Beckett places two pauses after the vital black
ball/white dog episode, pauses that prepare us for the "vision"
and the girl-in-the-punt memories, the two most important and
lyrically-charged passages in the falling action of the play.
Krapp's vision occurs on a "memorable night" in March when,
standing at the end of a jetty in the howling wind, he "saw the
whole thing", the "vision" which he wants to record this evening
before the "fire" (presumably the fire of creative intensity)
which enables him to shape his work dies out. This vision is,
however, never completely explained because Krapp twice switches
off the tape to wind it forward, thereby disrupting the explica-
tion of his staggering discovery. He does, however, hint that the
belief he has been going on for his entire life--the conviction
that he must keep the "dark" dimension of his life, especially
his creative life, under firm control--has been a tragically
limited and incorrect one. Indeed, Krapp subsequently attempts to
confess that the "dark" which he has "always struggled to keep
under" is, in reality, his most precious asset, a diverse tangle
of motifs, images, anecdotes and memories, many abrasive and
painful, stashed in his subconscious and charged with great
explosive potential.

Krapp's Vision Explained

Again Bair's book supplies the details which clarify Krapp's
vision, details deliberately omitted from the play. In chapter
fifteen, Bair traces one of Beckett's "late-nite prowls", a
journey to the end of a jetty in Dublin harbor during a severe
winter storm. Here Beckett is jolted by his "revelation"--a
"turning-point"--that (as he later confessed to Ludovic Janvier)
the "dark" he had struggled to repress was to become both the
catalyst and the raw material of his future creative activity.

Henceforth he would exploit the layers of memories in his Id, the grotesque and painful memories which he had steadfastly suppressed but which refused to go away.[17] To descend into the labyrinth of the self--this was to be the descent which would ignite future creative fires.

Impatiently refusing to listen to his remarks about how he might use the "light of his understanding" and the "fire" (presumably creative fire) to dissolve "storm and night" (chaos), Krapp switches off the tape and then winds it forward to the intimate passage beginning "--my face in her breasts and my hand on her." Then, before Krapp-at-39 can complete the sentence "Here I end--", the older Krapp switches off the machine and winds the tape back to the beginning of "my face in her breasts" sequence. In this passage Krapp is drifting in a boat down a stream which is flowing out of the upper lake with an unidentified woman (his sweetheart?) who is stretched out on the floorboards with her hands under her head and her eyes closed. After he tells his companion that the relationship is "hopeless", the exact word Krapp-at-29 used in breaking his relationship with Bianca, Krapp bends over the woman to shield her eyes, described as "slits", from the glaring sun and petitions: "Let me in."[18] This surprising request, coming so soon after his dismissal of the relationship as hopeless, reveals Krapp's desperate desire for a union, a sexual-spiritual conjunction, with another person. The woman's response is never given as the boat drifts in among the flags, stops, and is then moved gently "up and down" by the waves, action suggesting sexual activity and the rocking of a cradle by Mother Water.

Abruptly Krapp switches off the tape, broods for a moment, and then duplicates the banana-envelope-watch routine that began the drama. He also subsequently retreats into the backstage darkness where he again has three drinks, each drink separated by a ten-second delay. When he returns to the light, he moves "unsteadily" to the front of the table where he takes a "virgin" reel from the first drawer and places it on the machine. Taking his precious envelope from his pocket, he clears his throat and begins to record. This is Krapp's last tape and it begins with his angry assertion that he has "just been listening" to that "stupid bastard" I took myself for thirty years ago, a disclosure that enables the audience to fix old Krapp's age at 69 and to suspect that this day is another typical, let-us-review-the-year birthday ritual.

After lying to himself that he is thankful that he is "all done" with his foolish past, Krapp suddenly exclaims: "The eyes she had!"[19] Krapp-at-29 had praised Bianca's eyes and Krapp-at-39 had admired the "chrysolite" eyes of the dark, young beauty pushing the perambulator. Switching off the machine, Krapp insists that

40

"everything" was there in his sweetheart's eyes and then, after switching the machine back on, he indulges in a metaphysical conceit similar to those found in the love poems of John Donne and Andrew Marvell. Quickly Krapp associates his beloved's eyes (the microcosm) with the earth as globe (the macrocosm), the old "muckball" with all of its light and dark, the famine and feasting of the ages. Then, with quick candor, the elder Krapp condemns his earlier self for letting "that" (the relationship with the woman) go because it took his mind off his "homework." Just as quickly, Krapp, struggling to resolve his internal debate, reverses his field to rationalize that perhaps Krapp-at-39 was "right" in doing what he did, rejecting love in favor of his art.

After a brief glance at his envelope, Krapp admits that he has "nothing" to record and that his life now is the "sour cud" (indigestion) and the "iron stool" (commode?). He reveals that Effie, his opus magnum, sold only seventeen copies, and that he "crawled" out of his den once or twice before summer passed to sit shivering in the park, "drowned in dreams and burning to be gone."[20]

Yet Krapp reveals that his lust persists when he discloses that Fanny, a boney, old ghost of a whore whose name suggests anal sex, has come to visit him a "couple" of times, her sex being only slightly better than a kick in the crutch, the last word a pun for crotch. When Fanny asked how he managed sex at his age, Krapp replied that he had saved his sperm for her "all my life."

Rambling on, Krapp advises himself to finish his booze and to limp off to bed where he, propped up by a pillow, can remember what it was like to be alive as a young man in a world of color, motion and sound: gathering red-berried holly on Christmas in the wooded valley, riding Croghan and following the bitch dog through the Sunday morning haze, and pausing to listen to the church bells. After forcing himself to admit that he would like to "be again" because "once wasn't enough", Krapp suddenly tears his last tape from the machine, replacing it with the Krapp-at-39 tape which he winds forward to the girl-in-the-punt passage. The play then abruptly ends with complex irony. Krapp-at-39 is concluding his reel of tape (box three, spool five) by speculating that his best years offering a chance of happiness are gone, and yet he insists that he wouldn't want them back because of the "fire" (creative desire) in him now. Tragically, the fire in Krapp-at-39 drove him to choose literature over love but his great expectations were never realized with Effie. So Krapp-at-39 might hopefully insist that he does not want those years back: Krapp-at-69 has a different view. Looking back at his farewells to love and his unrealized artistic aspirations, he wants to "be again" but can't and so the play ends as the tape runs on in silence.

In <u>Krapp's Last Tape</u> "Now the day is over/Night is drawing nigh"
because Krapp, like so many of Beckett's people, is in the
painful evening of his life. More mobile than some of Beckett's
other protagonists, Krapp is nevertheless willing to remain in
his cluttered, restricted world where existence in the present is
made painful by the loud cries and quiet requests punctuating the
taped memories of the past. In inviting us to watch and to hear,
especially the latter, Krapp's increasingly drunken and disjointed odyssey into his past, Beckett gives us three Krapps: the
onstage Krapp-at-69, the disembodied voice of Krapp-at-39, and
the younger Krapp-at-29, thereby imparting a temporal dimension
to his monodrama. Each of the three Krapps is outwardly different
when we see them at different junctures on the time line which
Beckett has traced, but each is, both physically and psycho-
logically, basically the same man with the same chronic desires
which won't be denied: to eat, to drink, to make love and to
create. Amusingly, old Krapp can see the pompous, self-deluding
fool that he was at twenty-nine and thirty-nine; he has difficulty, however, seeing himself as the pariah and the self-
deceiving old man that he is now, a shrunken, sixty-nine-year-old
man who is both agitated by his present internal debate and by
the sounds surging out of the taped, zigzag patterns of his past.
Certainly Krapp has been forced to brood about and react to a
recurring question: "Should one reject affectionate but demanding
human relations in favor of art, an art that may bestow a limited
kind of immortality upon the artist?" At twenty-nine and thirty-
nine, Krapp made his decision, rejecting human involvement as
just so much "hopeless business" that took his mind off his
homework. And Krapp-at-69 seems to agree that Krapp-at-39 was
"right" in doing what he did, but this affirmation is very weak
and hollow and is preceded by a telling "perhaps". Moreover,
Krapp's final, chant-like reiterations of "Be again, be again"
demonstrate forcefully that he desires a second chance to relive
his life, a chance affording him another opportunity to establish
a joyful, reciprocal union with another person, especially
someone like the girl in the punt. Perhaps Krapp-at-69 now knows
that it is better to love than to create, especially if you are
an individual with limited creative powers.

A concentrated study of a man who has measured out his life with
banana skins, <u>Krapp's Last Tape</u> is enlivened by puns, a
Beckettian signature. The obvious pun in the title and Krapp's
numerous and joyful repetitions of the words "spool" and
"spooool" invite us to regard Krapp's life as both just so many
reels of tape and so many balls of waste--of just so much
collected, eroding matter. And Krapp's decay is, both literally
and symbolically, associated with the anus, with fecal matter,
and, in the references to the old whore Fanny, with buggery or
anal relations. Deliberately Krapp feasts on bananas which cause
constipation and thus he can retain and collect his excrement as

he retains and collects his tapes, a linkage that Beckett
underscores with the recurrent pun "spooool" and with the one
passage near the play's resolution where stool and spool are only
four words apart. Greedily hoarding the memories and the waste
material of his life, Krapp becomes a compulsive Collector Man, a
sequence of and an accumulation of the younger Krapps. Living in
a dim limbo land of half light and half shadow, a purgatory which
punishes those who rejected the favors of others, Krapp is just
that--a spool-and-stool man who is just so much excrement.

Krapp and Toilet Training

As a maverick man and a neurotic who collects his tapes and his
waste material, perhaps his excrement, Krapp's personality
problems may be traceable to his earlier years, specifically to
the years involving toilet training. As Sigmund Freud explains in
his theories about the stages of psychosexual development, a
child passes through three early sexual stages: the oral, the
anal, and the phallic. During this anal phase, which lasts from
about eighteen months to two and one-half years, the erogenous or
pleasurable zone shifts from the area of the child's mouth to the
anal area. In the anal-expulsive substage of this phase, the
child discovers that expelling the feces is a pleasurable
experience. So the child willingly defecates when the body
indicates that it is time, a biological process divorced from
larger, external circumstances. Later, however, complications
occur when the mother involves the child in toilet training, a
sequence involving obedience and control and a training program
which interferes with the child's pleasure-giving, excremental
activities. Resenting this interference with a bodily function
that gives pleasure, the child may rebel against this adult
desire for regulation, a rebellion that often results in fecal
retention. Moreover, as Freud suggests, if the conflict is not
satisfactorily resolved, the child's fecal retention and anal
fixation may broaden into a compulsive, persistent need to
collect and retain other possessions. As Paul R. Abramson
explains:

> The anal stage is ... the time during which
> stimulation is focused on eliminative functions
> through either holding back (anal retention) or
> letting go (anal expulsion) of the body's waste
> material. Freud believed that the child's response
> to toilet training (either conforming to it or
> opposing it) and his or her parents' reaction to
> this training have a profound influence on how the
> individual will respond to social pressures. Anal
> retentive types are presumed to adopt abstinent and
> stingy behaviors....[21]

43

Krapp's Last Tape suggests that Krapp is one of these anal
retentive types whose conflict with his mother, glimpsed in the
death watch scene by the weir, crippled his character. Moving
from anal fixation to abstinent and stingy behavior, Krapp became
a compulsive Collector Man. Frustrated and disappointed in his
efforts to achieve a Memorable Equinox, the proper blending of
light and dark or passion and creative accomplishment, Krapp
cultivated his growing addiction to booze and bananas, using the
bananas to prolong his constipation, a constipation hinting at
his deep-rooted desire to hoard his possessions and at his
long-standing, unresolved conflict with his mother in particular
and society in general. A withered, tormented old man whose
personality was profoundly influenced by the war with his mother,
Krapp is thus a grotesque neurotic with an anal fixation. Thus,
tangled in his tapes and surrounded by his shit, Krapp can only
eat another banana, brood about his lost chances for happiness,
and explode with anger when a sound from the past shatters the
precarious silence of his bleak and despairing present.

Another individual in the evening of his days, Yeat's Old Man is
also agitated--tormented--by his memories of a vanished past.
Emphasizing the ambivalence in the old man's character, Yeats
concentrates on the biological and historical legacies embodied
in the Old Man. On the biological level, the pedlar is a
"wretched foul old man" who is yet capable of moral awareness, an
abiding desire to release his mother's soul from torment. On the
historical level, the Old Man is an allegorical figure, an emblem
to remind us that Ireland has fallen into the hands of the
incompetent.[22] Like Beckett with his relentless experimentalism
and his steady pursuit of lessness--the bare bones of art--Yeats
also saw the challenge of the theatre as being one more concerned
with the management of words than with men. Rejecting irrevelant
movements and relishing vivid words, Yeats sought to link the
spoken word with restricted but revelatory patterns of conduct;
he sought, like Beckett, to devise a new form of drama that was
"distinguished, indirect, and symbolic"--a usable definition of
Purgatory and Krapp's Last Tape, two richly resonant dramas about
old men and their memories.

CHAPTER FOUR

PRELUDE

Father Figures in Modern Irish Drama

In her Saints, Scholars, and Schizophrenics: Mental Illness in
Rural Ireland, Nancy Scheper-Hughes points out that the traditional Irish family in Ballybran, her "model" village in County
Kerry in the west of Ireland, was, until the 1940's, patriarchal
with the household "overly controlled" by the father and "subtly
manipulated" by the mother. The father passed on his name, lands
and household property to the favorite (eldest) son, an action
which often forced the disinherited sons to seek employment in
distant towns or to emigrate. These fathers also used their
daughters "like pawns" in the moves preceding arranged marriages,
delaying decisions about dowry and inheritance rights so as to
prolong their control over their progeny. Menaced and manipulated by the greed of their fathers and the jealous possessive-
ness of their mothers, the daughters and sons in these Irish
families thus endured difficult lives, lives characterized by
drudgery, alienation, sexual repression, guilt, despair and, in
many instances, mental illness.

And it is the parsimonious patriarch--the grasping, brutal,
whiskey-sipping Father Figure--who appears and reappears in the
plays of modern Irish playwrights, plays recording the fragmentation of families. In Padraic Column's The Land (1905), a tyrant
father alienates his children with unreasonable regulations. In
T. C. Murray's Birthright (1910), a niggardly father's action
causes one of his sons to kill the other. In Louis D'Alton's The
Money Doesn't Matter (1941), Mannion, a good businessman whose
name suggests Mannon, drives his children to drink and death with
his obsession with wealth and social status. In Walter Macken's
Mungo's Mansion (1946), Mungo King, a crippled dock worker,
refuses to move his large family (eleven children) out of the
slum which is killing his youngest son. In his Vacant Possession
(1948), the Delaney family is evicted from an old house in Galway
because Gunner, the father, has spent the rent money on drink. In
his Home Is The Hero (1953), Paddo, a large hulk of a man,
returns home from a five-year stay in prison to terrify and
physically assault his wife and two children. In John B. Keane's
The Highest House on the Mountain (1961), Mikey Bannon, a
widower, sublimates his sexual urges into an obsessive concern
for food, and in his The Year of the Hiker (1962), the children
reject the dirty father who returns to his home after a twenty-
year absence. Finally, in Gone Tomorrow (1965), Tom Coffee traces
the faltering movement of Neil Dunne, an eighteen year old Irish

45

boy on the verge of manhood, who is misunderstood by his father, a play which anticipates Friel's first play.

Brian Friel's <u>Philadelphia</u>, <u>Here</u> <u>I</u> <u>Come</u> (1964) and Hugh Leonard's <u>Da</u> (1978) provide different responses to father figures and the resultant complications that often emerge from their action and inaction. These two plays are serious comedies designed to awaken thoughtful laughter (and nostalgia), gentle and sympathetic studies of the always shifting relationship between father and son, the latter play introducing one unique variation on the basic pattern, the father being only recently resurrected from his grave.

Chapter Four

Friel and Leonard: Fathers and Sons

> All the resources of the theatre--scene, colour,
> music, dance and movement--had to be brought into
> play: only a synthesis of the arts, supporting and
> highlighting the words, drawing attention to their
> value by allowing spaces between them, stretches of
> silence, unanswered questions, could hope to render
> anything like the complexity of the mind's proces-
> ses, its intuitions and fine shades of feeling, the
> whole undertow of the stream of consciousness.

> Katharine Worth, The Irish Drama
> of Europe From Yeats to Beckett

Certainly it is the "undertow of the stream of consciousness"
which challenges Brian Friel in Philadelphia, Here I Come (1964)
and Hugh Leonard in Da (1978), the first a three episode drama of
internal debate and fantasizing focusing on one son's imminent
departure from his home in Ireland, and the second a two act
drama of remembering focusing on another son's return, after many
years of absence in England, to his home in Ireland, a return
made necessary by his father's death. Evolving from the same
basic psychological matrix--the always awkward and ambivalent
father-son relationship--these two dramas strain to move beyond
the solid, restrictive borders of the proscenium frame, inching
away from the traditional formula of the realistic play in favor
of a fluid and flexible dramaturgy more apposite to the subjective reality which they investigate. While manifesting some
fidelity to the design, dress and devices of the conventional
rational-rhetorical-representational drama, these two psychological dramas push against and dissolve the solid walls of the
proscenium frame, mingle clock and psychological time, exploit
the endlessly suggestive magic of music, utilize dance, song and
the aside, use marionette-like movements, and, most significantly,
fragment the protagonist sons in both plays into two halves or
two selves, the one visible and the other invisible. Thus
Philadelphia and Da become, at intervals, complex dramas of
duality--of time present and time past--as the main characters
move abruptly from reality to reverie, from objective reality to
subjective dream and memory.

We know immediately that Philadelphia is to be a drama of duality
when we read Friel's description of Gar O'Donnell, the twenty-
five year old son caught in the routine drudgery of the small
village of Ballybeg in County Donegal, Ireland, a description
charged with the jargon--the nomenclature--of contemporary

47

psychology:

> The two Gars, Public Gar and Private Gar, are two
> views of the one man. Public Gar is the Gar that
> people see, talk to, talk about. Private Gar is the
> unseen man, the man within, the conscience, the
> alter ego, the secret thought, the id. / Private
> Gar, the spirit, is invisible to everyone, always.
> Nobody except Public Gar hears him talk. But even
> Public Gar, although he talks to Private Gar
> occasionally, never sees him and never looks at him.
> One cannot look at one's alter ego.[1]

Appropriately Private Gar makes his first appearance in the
opening moments of Episode I when Public Gar, weary from his last
long day of work among the dead fish in his father's general
store, retreats to the privacy of his bedroom to rest and to
speculate about his future life as a hotel worker in Philadelphia, U.S.A. As he reclines on his bed and broods about his
future, Private Gar suddenly erupts from the psyche of Public
Gar, giving physical dimension and a vigorous voice to the
reclining Gar's innermost fantasies. The extended sequence which
follows between the man within and the man without exposes all of
Public Gar's cherished and painful memories and secret dreams,
but chiefly his dreams of bold achievement or great renown like
those stirring in the timid soul of James Thurber's inept husband
in "The Secret Life of Walter Mitty". The reclining Gar's
fantasies include piloting, with "competent fingers", a "big,
bugger of a jet" which dives to machine gun an Irish fishing
boat, kicking the decisive goal for the Ballybeg soccer team,
riding the western plains of the U.S.A. as Gary the Kid, accepting a position with Patrick Palinakis, president of the biggest
chain of hotels in the world, performing as soloist the first
movement of the violin concerto in E minor, opus 64, by Jacob
Ludwig Felix Mendelssohn with an imaginary orchestra, teasing a
"gorgeous girl" as a "slick operator", imagining that he would
make a good president of the United States, chairman of General
Motors, boss of the Teamsters' Union, or member of the U.S.
Senate, or falling in love, as a handsome bachelor of forty-
three, with the lovely Tammara, the granddaughter of an exiled
Russian Prince.

This fantasy sequence is interrupted at frequent intervals by
Public Gar's conversations with Madge, the elderly housekeeper in
the O'Donnell home who is preparing his clothes for the trip, by
Gar's memories of sweet Katie Doogan, the girl he loved and lost,
by his examination of the Clarion , an old newspaper which falls
out of his suitcase he is taking and which records the date of
his parents' wedding, January 1, 1937, and by his unsuccessful
efforts to converse with his father who is concerned primarily

with ringing up sales in his general store. Later, in one significant scene near the end of Episode I, Public Gar sits in silence and stares across the table at his father during an evening meal while Private Gar, leaning against the wall and mimicking the posture and staccato syntax of a news commentator or the emcee at the grand celebrity ball, voices the frustration that Public Gar has experienced for most of his adult life with his undemonstrative father who just refuses to experiment with the English language:

> Screwballs, we've eaten together like this for the past twenty-odd years, and never once in all that time have you made as much as one unpredictable remark. Now...I'm leaving you forever. I'm going to Philadelphia to work in a hotel. And you know why I'm going, Screwballs....Because I'm twenty-five, and you treat me as if I were five....Because you pay me less than you pay Madge. But worse, far worse than that, Screwballs, because -- we embarrass one another....So tonight...I want you to make one unpredictable remark, and even though I'll still be on that plane tomorrow morning, I'll have doubts: Maybe I should have stuck it out; maybe the old codger did have feelings.[2]

As the silent father refuses to show his feeling and continues to eat his meal in silence, the hat which he wore all day in his store still on his head, Private Gar is compelled to dramatize, with harsh irony and scorn, Public Gar's anguish by tossing up his hands and exclaiming:

> Please, please don't cry, Screwballs; please don't say anything; and above all please don't stop eating. Just--just let me talk a bit more--let me communicate with someone--that's what they all advise--communicate--pour out your pent-up feelings into a sympathetic ear.[3]

Some Magical Moments While Fishing

Yet Public Gar, another young Irishman preparing to journey to America to seek his fortune because he can't endure "silent strong men", did share some magic moments of joyful communication and affectionate relation with his father, and the memory of a day spent fishing with his father on a lake keeps recurring in his flow of recollections, reminding one of a leitmotif in a musical composition. Speaking for Public Gar, Private Gar interrupts the evening prayers and leans over the father near the middle of Episode III, interrogating the praying father about this blue boat on-the-lake episode:

> God--maybe--Screwballs-behind those dead eyes and that
> flat face are there memories of precious moments in the
> past? ...Is it possible that you hoarded in the back of
> that mind of yours--do you remember--it was an after-
> noon in May--oh, fifteen years ago--I don't remember
> every detail but some things are as vivid as can be:
> the boat was blue and the paint was peeling..and the
> left rowlock kept slipping and you had given me your
> hat and had put your jacket round my shoulders because
> there had been a shower of rain. And between us at that
> moment there was this great happiness, this great
> joy...it was a great, great happiness, an active,
> bubbling joy--although nothing was being said--just the
> two of us fishing on a lake on a showery day--and...I
> knew that this was precious and your hat was soft on
> the top of my ears...and then, for no reason at all
> except that you were happy too, you began to sing:

> All round my hat I'll wear a green coloured ribbono,
> All round my hat for a twelve month and a day,
> And if anybody asks me the reason why I wear it,
> It's all because my true love is far, far away.[4]

Later, the evening prayers completed, Public Gar asks his father
near the close of Episode II if he remembers this blue boat-
fishing excursion when "you put your jacket round my shoulders
and gave me your hat."[5] When the father replies that he can't
recall the episode--the blue boat or his singing "All Round My
Hat I'll Wear a Green Coloured Ribbon"--the Public Gar fran-
tically cries out with exasperation: "It doesn't matter. Forget
it."[6]

Ironically the father--stoical store-owner and county councillor
S. B. O'Donnell--does have one cherished memory of interacting
and holding hands with his son, but it is a different memory than
the blue boat one, and he belatedly confesses it to the wrong
person--Madge--when it is too late to mitigate his son's mental
suffering or to alter his plan for departure. The father's memory
concerns Public Gar's response to his first days of school, and
the father recounts it with loving exactness:

> D'you mind the trouble we had keeping him at school
> just after he turned ten....I can hear him saying...
> I'm not going to school. I'm going into my daddy's
> business...You tried to coax him to go to school,
> and not a move you could get out of him, and...this
> wee sailor suit as smart looking on him, and--and--
> and at the heel of the hunt I had to go with him

50

myself, the two of us, hand in hand, as happy as
larks--we were that happy, Madge--and him dancing
and chatting beside me.[7]

Predictably, it is the village schoolmaster--Master Boyle--who
responds to Public Gar's impending departure like a father losing
a son. A white-haired, handsome and defiant sixty-year old man
and a sometime poet, Boyle enters near the end of Episode I to
lecture Public Gar on the rightness of his action:

> You're doing the right thing of course. You'll never
> regret it. I gather it's a vast restless place that
> doesn't give a curse about the past; and that's the
> way things should be. Impermanence and anonymity--it
> offers great attractions.[8]

Advising the young man about the folly of always "looking back"
over his shoulders, Boyle then surprises Public Gar by giving him
a small book of his poems, and he later embarrasses the young man
when he embraces him briefly before he departs, the kind of
response Public Gar was looking to receive from his silent
father. Thus encouragement, a gift and an act of affection come
from an unexpected source in this small village where silence is
the barrier separating son from father and father from son.

Unable and unwilling to endure further the daily drudgery in the
store, his father's silence, and "all this loneliness, this
groping, this dreadful bloody buffoonery" in Balleybeg, described
by the angry Public Gar as a "quagmire, a backwater, a dead-end"
near the end of Episode II, Public Gar will flee his village the
following morning on a "big bugger" of a jet and, yet, as his
final speech indicates, he will run and rerun the "film" of his
village and its inhabitants which he has in his head, distilling
his memories of all "coarseness" until all that is left is
"precious, precious gold."

The externalization of memory and subconscious desire is also
the major concern of Hugh Leonard in Da, another memory play
revolving around the actions, some physical but mostly mental, of
another son, the forty-two year old Charlie Tynan, who has
returned to his home near Dun Laoghaire in Ireland to sort
through some papers and some memories following the death of his
eighty-four year old father who spent virtually all of his life
working as a gardener for a wealthy Anglo-Irish family. And using
the same successful technique that Friel employed in
Philadelphia, Leonard splits his major character into two
halves--Charlie Now and Young Charlie--thereby facilitating
Charlie Now's interaction with the memory of his former self, a
verbal fencing match that continues throughout the play and

51

contributes an assortment of revealing vignettes from the Tynan family album.

Like Friel, Leonard also indicates in his stage directions that his play is to move back and forth between reality and reverie, between time present and time past. Locating his play in the kitchen of the Tynan home which he describes as "the womb of the play", Leonard adds that the action takes place in "May, 1968 and, later, times [and places] remembered." After an opening segment of action showing Charlie Now, still dressed in the overcoat he wore to the funeral, sorting letters, family papers and old photos into two piles on the kitchen table and reminiscing with Oliver, a former friend who has come to offer his condolences, the dead Da, dressed in his Sunday best, suddenly appears, his appearance suggesting a ghost refusing to remain in his grave but, in actuality, just a disturbing memory in Charlie Now's head. The son's anger is visible in his response to this unwelcome visitor-apparition:

> Now will you get out and leave me be. You're dead.
> You're in Dean's Grange, in a box, six feet under...
> with her. I carried$_9$you...it's over, you're gone, so
> get out of my head.

Da As Irish Fury

Yet the dead Da refuses to get out of his son's head, haunting him and pursuing him like a tenacious Irish Fury and forcing him to re-live and re-examine his past life: his angry and impatient responses to his mother who rescued him—a frail, abandoned ten-day old baby—from the Holles Street Hospital, a prelude to his later adoption; his joyful acceptance of a job as a filing clerk earning forty-five shillings a week in the firm directed by Mr. Drumm, a thin, acerbic cynic; his awkward advances toward Mary Tate, known locally as the Yellow Peril, near the sea; his unsuccessful attempt to take Da to live with him in England after his wife died; his sarcastic remarks to Mrs. Prynne, Anglo-Irish owner of the great Enderly house and gardens, who gives Da the news of his pension (twenty-six pounds per annum) and twenty-five pounds when he is dismissed from his post as gardener after fifty-four years of loyal service; his departure to Belgium for his marriage; and his anxiety when the retired Da, after smashing a buxom female attendant in the stomach with his fist, escapes from the hotel for elderly people where Charlie Now had placed him by climbing over a wall.

While Charlie Now is time-tripping and reliving his various experiences with Da, he is also fencing with Young Charlie, another memory with great expectations and a caustic tongue.

Unlike the ego-alter ego arrangement in Friel's play where Public Gar never looks at or sees Private Gar, Charlie Now interacts repeatedly with Young Charlie, an extended sequence that begins early in Act I when Young Charlie, who often retreats to the lavatory to read his books, first appears as a shabbily dressed, seventeen year old "bookworm" chafing against parental directives. Denouncing his earlier self as a "little prick", Charlie Now insults and lectures Young Charlie, correcting his pronunciation and condemning his softness, swift jibes that create a charged feeling of mutual contempt between the two. When Young Charlie expresses his disgust with his deferential parents who "always crawl" before those of higher social standing, Charlie Now is forced to admit that "the shame of being ashamed of them was the worst part, wasn't it?"[10]

Later, in the opening moments of Act II, the pattern of action is reversed as Young Charlie verbally attacks Charlie Now as a very "ordinary" forty year old who is too fond of drink, a smart Alec with "everything behind him and nothing to look forward to."[11] Contending that the older Charlie is "jizzless", Young Charlie condemns his flippancy and inertia:

> Everything's a laugh, isn't it? I see who's your age...same thing. All lah-de-dah and make a joke of it. God if something good happens to me, I jump up in the air, I let out a yell, I run. Your sort just sits there.[12]

His self-esteem jolted, Charlie Now quickly counterattacks to put down his young adversary:

> Don't get righteous with me, my pasty-faced little friend. It doesn't become you. Were you any good? Who was it once gave him a packet of six razor blades for Christmas?[13]

Yet the major portion of the play's time is reserved for Charlie Now's zig-zagging conversation--a shouting match at intervals--between Charlie Now and Da. In one Act One scene very similar to the evening meal episode between Public Gar O'Donnell and his father in Philadelphia, Charlie Now studies his father's face and asks himself if this man, who worked for fifty-eight years, nine hours a day, in a garden so steep a horse couldn't climb it, ever nurtured any special dreams:

> All those years you sat and looked into the fire. What went through your head? What did you think of? What thoughts? I never new you to have a hope or a dream or say a half-wise thing.[14]

Da does, however, retain some special memories, most of them spiraling around his wife Margaret, the lovely young girl with "shiny bright hair" who reminded him of the heroines in "the story books", but it is Charlie Now who has one memory that refuses to go away or to lose its vividness, the memory of a day's outing on Dalkey Hill that is quite similar to the father-son, blue boat episode in Philadelphia. Only seven years of age and respectfully regarding his father as "an Einstein", Young Charlie walks hand-in-hand with his father, who is affectionately yelling commands to their dog Blackie, toward Dublin Bay, the two of them laughing and singing "Waxie Dargle". Helping his son up over the rocks near the shore, Da praises the "fine mackrel sky", boasts of what they will do when they win the Irish Sweepstakes, points out the Kish lightship in and a vessel departing from Dublin Bay, lectures his young son on how to treat women properly, smokes his pipe, and assures his son that he will protect him from ghosts. Finally, when Da agrees to take his seven-year old son home because he is afraid of the approaching evening darkness, the Young Charlie blurts out: "Da, I love you."[15]

There are no village school masters giving advice to a young man like Master Boyle in Philadelphia, but Mr. Drumm is, in many ways, his counterpart in Da. Conducting an extended catechism, Drumm repeatedly lectures Young Charlie on how to succeed in life, admonitions that urge Charlie to reject his father and the world of deferential, mindless, menial servitude which he inhabits. Describing Da as Charlie's "enemy", a man too ignorant to feel pain, Drumm adds:

> There are millions like him: inoffensive, stupid, and not a damn bit of good. They've never said no in their lives or to their lives, and they'd cheerfully see the rest of us buried. If you have any sense, you'll learn to be frightened of him.[16]

Yet Charlie Now later discovers that his father is not that easily cast off. Years after Young Charlie has quit his job at Drumm's firm, a dreary thirteen-year ordeal of stashing folders in filing cabinets, and has gone to live in England as a writer, he is haunted by the memory of his father as in this episode in a fashionable restaurant:

> Long after I'd quit the job and seen the last of Drumm, I was dining out in London: black dickie-bow, oak paneling...the sort of place where you have to remember not to say thanks to the waiters. I had just propelled an erudite remark across the table... when I felt a sudden tug....I looked, and there you were....Paring your corns, informing me that bejasus the weather would hold up if it didn't rain, and

sprinkling sugar on my bread when Ma's back was
turned.[17]

And the conclusion of Da suggests that the father will continue
to reappear in his son's flow of thoughts despite the son's
vigorous efforts to exorcise him. Insisting that the "debt is
cancelled", Charlie Now tears the black armband from his overcoat
and then taps his head: "I'm turning you out. Of here. See
that?"[18] Responding to his son's decisive action, Da informs his
son that it isn't easy to "get rid of a bad thing", and that he
is now willing to return with him to London. Furious at this
suggestion, Charlie Now grabs his case packed with papers and
sprints through the door, pausing only to lock the front door and
to throw away the key. Seconds later Da walks through the fourth
wall and follows his son in his march away from the house while
singing a verse of "Waxy Dargle", concluding action that indicates that Da, as recurring memory, will, indeed, return with his
son to London.

Memory Plays with Additional Dimensions

As memory dramas attempting to chase down and reflect large
segments of elusive, subjective experience, these two plays
understandably explore new dimensions for the traditional,
realistic domestic drama. Friel's Philadelphia is clearly less
experimental than Leonard's Da as Friel restricts most of his
play's action to the solid, circumstantial clutter of the kitchen
and Gar's bedroom in the O'Donnell home. Yet Gar's bedroom, often
in darkness, becomes a special sanctuary where voices resound as
in an "echo-chamber" and where the id can break free of the
powerful control of Gar's ego. Moreover, music, song and dance
enrich Friel's play by providing special evocative intensity for
several episodes. For example, when Public Gar first appears on
stage, he "marches" vigorously in singing "Philadelphia, Here I
Come" with "joy and excitement." He later sings the same song in
a duet with his soon-to-arrive private self, the Private Gar
singing alternate lines in the darkness offstage. Later in
Episode I, a recording of the first movement of Mendelssohn's
violin concerto provides the sound track for Public Gar as he
preens, flexes his fingers, adjusts his bow tie and prepares for
his solo performance with an imaginary orchestra. Still later in
Episode I, Public Gar attempts to escape his melancholy thoughts
about the mother he never knew by replacing Mendelssohn with a
lively piece of Ceilidhe Band music, music that sends him off on
a leaping, frenzied dance around his bedroom. Private Gar also
hums trumpet fanfare during the long evening meal ordeal before
he switches to the unctuous tones of a "commentator at a manne-
quin parade."

Episode II opens with Public Gar, again lying on his bed, singing
a love song about his beloved assuring him that it will "not be
long" before their wedding day. Private Gar, who has been dozing
in a chair, responds by lilting a "mad air" of his own making,
and by then singing a verse from "Give the Woman in Bed More
Porter", singing intended to arouse Public Gar from his meditative melancholy. Later, in the final scene in Episode II, Public
Gar, overcome with sorrow at saying farewell to Katie Doogan,
attempts to whistle "Philadelphia, Here I Come" but he is only
able to whistle the first phrase before the notes die away.

Friel uses music and song to complement and accelerate Private
Gar's anguish in Episode III. Private Gar sings the first verse
of "All Round My Hat" to the heedless, praying S. B. O'Donnell in
the opening moments of this act, a song the old man later denies
singing. Later, Private Gar, his head lowered, his foot tapping,
his fingers clicking in syncopated rhythm, sings a snatch of
"Should Old Acquaintance Be Forgot" as a mocking commentary on
the checker match between S. B. O'Donnell and the Canon as Public
Gar mimes his action in the bedroom. Seconds later Private Gar
asks for Mendelssohn's second movement of the violin concerto,
music which prompts Private Gar, now in a frenzy, to thrust his
face between the two men at the checkerboard who, of course,
can't see him or respond to his rapid barrage of questions.
Appropriately no music or singing is heard in the final moments
of Friel's play as Public Gar struggles to keep firm in his
resolve to depart from his home of twenty·five years.

Like Friel, Leonard also locates most of the action of his play
in the kitchen-living room of the Tynan home, but he arranges the
remaining regions of the stage so as to provide quick transitions
in time and space, transitions so necessary to a drama tracing
the kaleidoscopic shiftings of a son remembering his past. For
example, there are two areas on either side of the kitchen and a
series of connecting steps and ramps which climb up and over the
kitchen. One of these two areas beside the kitchen is used for
the seafront episodes and includes a park bench and, later, an
ornamental bench. Behind this seafront area, on rising platforms,
is the hilltop region later visited by Da and Young Charlie. At
the other side of the kitchen is a neutral area, defined by
changing lighting, and it is here that the angry exchange between
Young Charlie and Mr. Drumm in Drumm's office occurs.

The promenade scene between Mr. Drumm and Young Charlie, the
job-seeker, occurs in the seafront area early in Act I as the
sound of sea gulls and the music of the Artane Boys Marching Band
are heard offstage. The Young Charlie-Mary Tate interaction also
occurs in the same area, an interaction referred to by Leonard as
"ritual, laconic and fast." During this sequence Young Charlie
and Oliver sing together a verse from the song "Lily Marlene".

56

After Young Charlie rejects Mary to flee to the safety of a billiard hall, she chants "Daddy's little baby" before she gives way to weeping. The dismissal scene involving Da and Mrs. Prynne also occurs in this same area. And crossing the invisible barriers and walking through the non-existent walls that ostensibly separate these various stage areas is the persistent Da, the "forelock-tugging old crawler", who sings again and again snatches of the song "Waxie Dargle" to the tune of "The Girl I Left Behind Me".

Successful domestic dramas that exploit the running conflict between two two-man debate teams--Public/Private Gar and Young Charlie/Charlie Now--Philadelphia, Here I Come and Da trace one son's reaction to a living father who won't talk and another son's reaction to his dead foster-father who won't shut up. Using and improving upon the basic techniques of the conventional domestic drama, these two plays successfully record the protagonists' abrupt movement from reality to reverie and memory, thereby giving form and motion and substance to the powerful urges that ripple through the subterranean habitations of consciousness of two Irish sons involved in the process of discovering new meanings for the words father and home.

Pirandello, Williams and Leonard

In retrospect one can view Philadelphia, Here I Come and Da as two dramas that strain to move beyond dramatic photography, but Leonard, with greater boldness and creativeness, is far more successful in his attempt to transform and transcend the mundane in Da than Friel is in Philadelphia, Here I Come. Friel is too tentative; he is not, finally, ·able to break away from the realism that is the trademark of most of his plays, plays that provide us with portraits--not in depth but in sharp focus--of village folk. Thus Friel is not a profound writer in this early play but his limitations are inherent in his method.

Yet Leonard is a different case altogether. Leonard obviously knew that his break with realism in Da was absolutely necessary because he was arranging a memory play, and this genre's basic premise is the subjectivity of modern relativism. It is not the world of clock but of psychological time. The wistful, painful and comic memories of the son in Da could not be embodied successfully with the solidities of the naturalistic stage. Thus the transparent house, the quick transitions from time present to time past, and the use of light and music to isolate and throw into bold relief characters, certain objects and events--all these are the techniques that an imaginative playwright knows he must employ in a play which is basically the record of an inner experience.

So with Leonard it is not what happened but how an individual
feels about what happened that is vital. Accepting the memory
play premise, Leonard thus avoids the chain of causality--the
predictable linkage of episode--so easy to follow in Friel's
play. Thus the plot of Da is finally little more than a tenuously
coherent sequence of episodes from the past, scenes tracing the
son's irritated interaction with his foster parents with their
routine existence and limited vistas. With its elusive, pastel,
quickly dissolving, nostalgic reminiscences, Da is, therefore,
firmly in the tradition of the psycho-drama established by
Strindberg and Pirandello and later practiced by Tennessee
Williams, especially in The Glass Menagerie. In fact, Leonard
would readily agree with one aspect of Williams' artistic theory
which appears in the "Production Notes" to The Glass Menagerie:

> Everyone should know nowadays the unimportance of
> the photographic in art: that truth, life, or
> reality is an organic thing which the poetic
> imagination can represent or suggest, in essence,
> only through transformation, through changing into
> other forms than those which are merely present in
> appearance.[19]

Hence it is Leonard's insightful, premeditated intent to capture
the erratic flow of what Katharine Worth describes as the "undertow of the stream of consciousness" that determines the design of
Da, a memory play possessing the fluid form of its content.
Leonard takes greater risks but he manages to write a play with
greater subtlety, mood range and hypnotic power than Friel's, a
play successfully exposing the labyrinth of a son's subjective
experience while achieving a laudable marriage of form and
content.

PRELUDE

Incompatible Couples in Modern Drama

When Ibsen, the master builder, published A Doll's House in 1879, he brought new finesse and controversy to the drama of domestic discord with its incompatible couples that Molière and Shakespeare had exploited before him. Exposing the powerful social pressures that a woman faced in an exclusively masculine society with laws devised by men and with a judicial system that judged feminine conduct from a masculine point of view, Ibsen studied the eight year marriage of Nora and Torvald Helmer. A pompous, priggish lawyer who never doubts his masculine superiority, Torvald has never "once sat down seriously and tried to get to the bottom of anything" with his wife. Regarding his wife as a "feather-head," Torvald expects her to surrender her individuality to the established domestic and conjugal obligations. She is his helpmate, the dainty dancing figure and the charming little mother--three roles that fix and identify, in his view, her functions and her character. Hence Nora is a performer and not a person in her own home: a "little squirrel" who surreptitiously eats forbidden macaroons, or a bird-bride who twitters like a "little skylark," reductive analogies that suggest that Nora is more animal-bird than human.

Yet behind Nora's naiveness, her sense of mischief, her rapport with children, and her pride in her cleverness is an intelligence and courageous resourcefulness which her husband can't recognize. So because of her affection for Torvald she commits forgery to save his career. Yet when he fails to appreciate fully and applaud her bold action, an action requiring some courage in a reactionary community where appearances must be maintained at all cost, Nora knows she must leave her doll's house because she has been living with a stranger for eight years.

Like Nora Helmer, Crystal also discovers that she has been living with a stranger in Brian Friel's Crystal and Fox, a drama of menace and masks which D.E.S. Maxwell refers to as a chiaroscuro whose manner is naturalistic. As vigilant but puzzled pragmatist who refuses to leave her husband's side, Crystal is aware from the outset of her mate's destructive plan to disperse and destroy their circus family. Like Nora, Crystal also compromised and adjusted, assuming the mask of the trusting, loyal wife and helper in order to keep the relationship intact. Yet, like Nora, Crystal finally scrambles away from her duplicitious mate and his endless actors' patois when, in the play's resolution, she catches a terrifying glimpse of the depravity--the complex tangle of dark motives--behind Fox's controlled exterior and compulsive conduct. Thus Crystal realizes, with sudden, painful explosiveness, that she can no longer live with an undeviating, monster-man who would sacrifice anyone and anything to obtain his vision, a vision emerging out of what William Butler Yeats might refer to as the "testy delirium" of a sick and sinister man with an active imagination.

Dan Rooney is the man-as-monster in Samuel Beckett's <u>All That Fall</u> and it is Maddy Rooney's misfortune to be married to this human computer who, disregarding her questions, her casual comments and her sincere concern for his well-being, shuts out his wife and his associates by remaining silent or by solving mathematical puzzle-problems. How Maddy could love her unresponsive mate is but one of several riddles in Beckett's play about two aged, world-weary travelers whose talk--or lack of it--defines them.

Chapter Five

Friel's <u>Crystal</u> <u>and</u> <u>Fox</u> and Beckett's <u>All</u> <u>That</u> <u>Fall</u>: the Odd
Couples in Fable and Parable

On a hot Summer's day a fox was strolling through an
orchard till he came to a bunch of Grapes just ripening
on a vine which had been trained over a lofty branch.
'Just the thing to quench my thirst,' quoth he. Drawing
back a few paces, he took a run and a jump, and just
missed the bunch. Turning round again with a One, Two,
Three, he jumped up, but with no greater success. Again
and again he tried after the tempting morsel, but at
last had to give up, and walked away with his nose in
the air, saying: 'I am sure they are sour.'

'It is easy to despise what you cannot get.'

Aesop's "The Fox and the Grapes"

A two-act play compartmentalized into six separate episodes,
Brian Friel's fifth play, <u>Crystal</u> <u>and</u> <u>Fox</u>, has been accepted by
most viewers/readers as a realistic drama with allegorical names
tracing the decline and disintegration of a shabby and shoddy
traveling acting company (The Fox Melarkey Show) which is working
the towns and villages in the west of contemporary Ireland, a
disintegration deliberately brought about by the premeditated,
ruthless and obsessive scheming of Fox Melarkey, the proprietor
of this itinerant show. Yet <u>Crystal</u> <u>and</u> <u>Fox</u> is much more than
mere realistic reporting because Friel has embellished and
intensified the play's rough-edged versimilitude by incorporating
characters, animals, suggestive individual episodes and segments
of action from well-known folk tales into the text of his play.
Basically <u>Crystal</u> <u>and</u> <u>Fox</u> resurrects with significant, ironical
variations the protagonist, the narrative sequence and the moral
argument of the medieval beast fable "The Fox and the Grapes"
which identifies Reynard, the fox, as the personification of
cunning. In this didactic beast fable Reynard exhausts all of his
wiles and most of his energy to obtain the glistening grapes
which are hanging just beyond his reach. Defeated in all of his
efforts to claim this fruit, Reynard finally concludes that the
grapes did not merit all this effort because they were "sour", a
conclusion emphasizing the idea that man habitually ridicules and
rejects those objectives which he cannot achieve.

Bestowing additional dimensions of meaning upon Friel's play are
segments of speech and action and archetypal arrangements of
setting from "Little Red Riding-Hood", the folk song "A-hunting
We Will Go" from "The Farmer in the Dell" and the Biblical story
of the prodigal son, fragments focusing upon the beautiful young

61

woman (a "princess" in this play) awaiting rescue, the returned
son, the magical number three, and the dream-inspired search for
an earthly paradise. Yet Friel adroitly fuses and alters what he
borrows from these folk tales with their compromises and happy
endings coming after flights from evil beings through dark
forests, ironically deflecting and inverting many of the ramifi-
cations of these tales so that he may trace the career of a man
obsessed with his dream, a dream involving a return to Edenic
innocence and delight when he and his loved one, then much
younger and devoid of all cares, danced joyfully along lanes and
on beaches in glorious sunshine.

The man in relentless pursuit of his dream in the play is Fox
Melarkey, a small, narrow-shouldered, lightly built, fifty-year-
old man with the lean, sallow and angular face of a fox, a face
stamped with a network of shallow wrinkles and "with age since
childhood." Like his legendary counterpart in the beast fable,
Fox is the wrinkled, vigilant young man grown old and cynical too
soon, the animal-man who relies upon stealth and cunning to
survive. As an experienced actor and stage manager, Fox has spent
his entire life in and around gambling tables, side shows, fairs
and theatres and hence is an accomplished performer. When menaced, Fox uses his flexible face; his "eyes go flat" and expres-
sionless and he retreats behind a "mask of bland simplicity and
vagueness." A seemingly tireless, restless, agile man and a glib
liar, Fox is a mercenary, resourceful con man who unfeelingly
manipulates and discards others to reach his goals, a discon-
tented schemer with quick, automatic responses for virtually
every person in every contingency. Moreover, his last name
reinforces the implications of the first because Melarkey is
obviously a pun, an altered spelling of the slang word "malarkey"
which means insincere speech.

Yet Fox was apparently not always a skillful opportunist repeating insincere speeches. In episode two of act one, a Goldilocks
and the Three Vans episode crowded with animals, vehicles, motifs
and people recurrent in the world's folklore, he remembers an
earlier, glorious spring day when, cycling with wide-eyed wonder
near the town of Drung in County Tyrone in pursuit of his fortune, he encountered a caravan with three white horses and three
golden vans:

> No, no, my love; it was the twelfth day of a glorious
> May. And the Fox was cycling out to make his fortune in
> the world with nothing but his accordion and his
> rickety wheel and his glib tongue, when what did he spy
> at the edge of the road but three snow-white horses and
> three golden vans.[1]

62

Looking down from his cycle like a knight from his horse, Fox peers into the first and second golden vans but finds nothing. Dismounting, he finds an old man, a "snow-white mare" named Alice and a "princess" beside the third van, a princess wearing a brooch, a blue blouse, a navy skirt, and a royal-blue ribbon in her hair. Whipping off his cap and bowing low before her, Fox addresses the princess: "What big eyes you've got."[2] When the princess responds quickly to his energetic gallantries by falling to her feet, Fox marries this princess named Crystal and goes into business with her father. Remembering this remarkable experience on a May day when the air was perfumed with the smell of heather, Fox admits that he then had "more hope than courage."

Crystal seems at first to be the appropriate name for this radiant, young woman taken away from her aging father by the fortune-seeking Fox because Crystal, a name visible in various folktales, has connotations of clarity and brightness as expressed in the folk adage "As clear as crystal." Moreover, Crystal is the word used to refer to a transparent quartz or rock crystal which exhibits a definite and symmetrical internal structure with geometrically arranged cleavage plans and external faces. Friel's description of Fox's wife deliberately invites us to view her as a piece of human crystal, a tall, young woman with a "well-structured" face and a "fresh and honest attractiveness" which shines forth after grooming. Yet Fox is later to discover to his dismay that Crystal is not as transparent -- as naive, sincere and virtuous -- as she appears. She has a "definite internal structure" which manifests itself when her son Gabriel returns from wandering the world and when Fox confesses to her in the surprising resolution of the play, and this "internal struc-ture" is neither clear nor clean but soiled and "rotten." Later discussion of the final Crystal-Fox confrontation, an ordeal of confessing and testing jolting both participants, will demon-strate the evil hidden behind Crystal's fresh, honest face.

Attended by his young princess-wife and driven by his youthful hopefulness, Fox gradually acquires the trucks, wagons, tents, stage properties, animals and actors necessary for the successful operation of a touring acting company. And he is successful: his group acquires a reputation and is invited to perform before large, demonstrative audiences in many of the large towns in Ireland. As Pedro, the sixty-year-old dog trainer in the troup, explains:

> Eight -- ten years ago -- My God (with genuine enthu-
> siasm and pride), he was on top of his form then!
> Cracking jokes, striding about, giving orders like a
> king; and everywhere he went, Gabby perched up there on
> top of his shoulders! My God, the Fox Melarkey Show was
> a real show then![3]

Fox Detests Yahoos

Yet as the years pass Fox's interest in the daily, monotonous routine -- "same conversations, same jokes, same yahoo audiences" -- of the acting company diminishes. A violent quarrel with his son Gabriel, who departs in bitterness, also contributes to the company's steady decline, a decline more and more visible in the reduced number of actors, the holes in the equipment, the broken seats, the defective truck, and in the smaller audiences in the smaller villages where the yokels stomp and yell to interrupt the troupe's ragged performance of their romantic drama, "The Doctor's Story", an erratically timed, sentimental sequence enacted by inept performers with stage names like El Cid and Tanya.

Still later when the son Gabriel, fleeing from his debts and crimes and the psychiatrists and the police in England, rejoins the company after a five-year absence, Fox confesses to his son that he has "changed" drastically and that he is now exceedingly "weary" of deceiving people with false faces and false facts:

> Weary of all this ... this making-do, of conning people that know they're being conned. Sick of it all. Not sick so much as desperate; desperate for something that ... that has nothing to do with all this. Restless, Gabby boy, restless. And a man with a restlessness is a savage bugger.[4]

When Gabriel subsequently asks his father why he is so restless and desperate, Fox replies that he wants to experience a death-rebirth sequence, a death-departure from the onerous circus routine and a life-rebirth entry into a "heaven" with his wife:

> What do I want? I want .... I want a dream I think I've had to come true. I want to live like a child. I want to die and wake up in heaven with Crystal.[5]

Disenchanted, restless and tormented by a dream he thinks he has had, Fox has already set in motion his plan to destroy the company he has built so that he can realize his dream of living like a child with Crystal on the roads. He deliberately provokes El Cid and Tanya, Cid's wife, by refusing to give them the last curtain call after each performance, an adamant ploy which El Cid refers to as humiliating, like being "spit on by a weasel." When El Cid and his wife subsequently leave Fox's company to join the Dick Prospect group, El Cid denounces Fox as a devious man who is "twisted as a bloody corkscrew", a treacherous man who will not rest until he has "ratted" on everyone in his company.

Thus El Cid, more of a magician than an actor, is forced to
discover that his "limited talent" does not match his "limitless
optimism"; he is not, like his Spanish namesake, an epic hero, a
gallant warrior destined to swagger successfully through a
dangerous world. Nor is Tanya the exotic, lovely heroine her name
suggests. Rather, both have been reduced to playing parts in a
wretched melodrama with its stereotypical mother superior,
beatific nun (Sister Petita Sancta) and handsome, compassionate
doctor, a meretricious world far removed from their private
dreams of glorious achievement and from the heroic Spanish world
of high adventure and romance. The ironic discrepancy between
what one can imagine and what one is forced to endure, the
central thesis in this disconcerting tragedy, is thus reiterated
in the careers of El Cid and Tanya, a subordinate plot complication operating as a muted complement to the Crystal-Fox major
plot complication.

Distressed at the departure of El Cid and Tanya, a departure that
threatens the play's future success and that takes twenty minutes
from the variety show, Crystal asks Fox to explain his conduct:

> Without Cid! Without Tanya! What's got into you? Last
> month it was Billy Hercules. And before that it was the
> Fritter twins. Fox, I'm asking you.[6]

Yet Fox refuses to respond candidly to his wife's entreaties (his
brief replies are riddles), and he also refuses to alter his
conduct which is alienating and driving away the remaining
members of the troupe. His dream has mesmerized him and so he
next poisons Gringo, Pedro's dog, a cruel deed that stuns the old
man who later leaves to wander the roads in debilitating despair.
Challenged openly by his astonished son Gabriel who argues that
his "crazy scheme" is "wrecking the show", Fox replies:

> Once, maybe twice in your life, the fog lifts, and you
> get a glimpse, an intuition; and suddenly you know that
> this can't be all there is to it -- there has to be
> something better than this.[7]

The "something better" which Fox caught a glimpse of in his
intuitive, visionary experience is finally explained to Crystal
in episode five of Act Two, a revelation deliberately synchron-
ized with the coming of dawn, the dawn following the arrest of
Gabriel by an Irish policeman and two English detectives. [The
detective named Coalstream plans to "cool off" Gabriel.] This
"something better" is Fox's glowing memory of a joyful sequence
he shared with his wife thirty years ago in and near a channel of
water flowing into the sea a few miles north of Galway. Only two
weeks married at the time, they responded to Crystal's "mad
notion" of going for a swim at dawn, an impulse that sent them

racing across the wet fields and into the channel where they splashed around in the midst of hundreds of flat fish which were wriggling under their feet. After Crystal, shrieking with laughter, falls into the freezing water, she pulls Fox down to join her, a ceremonial baptism that inspires Fox to "leap about like a monkey" and to tie a plait of seaweed in his wife's hair. Afterwards they danced on the sand and relaxed in the sun, behaving like two young pilgrims who had crossed a stream of water to get to their land of joy, their heaven.

Inspired by his detailed description of this precious memory, a recall and recitation that fills both Crystal and himself with "warmth and obvious joy", Fox affirms that he will accelerate their return to this sun-splashed world of joyful innocence and glad, animal movements by immediately selling the company:

> Don't you worry. I'll get rid of it. And when I do there'll just be you and me and the old accordion and the old rickety wheel -- all we had thirty years ago, remember? You and me. And we'll laugh again at silly things and I'll plait seaweed into your hair again. And we'll go only to the fairs we want to go to, and stop only at the towns we want to stop at, and eat when we want to eat, and lie down when we feel like it. And everywhere we go, we'll know people and they'll know us -- 'Crystal and Fox.'[8]

Fox Has Glimpsed the Grapes

Like his red-faced companion in the beast fable, Fox has glimpsed the grapes which he must have, and the falling action of Friel's play traces the decisive steps which he takes to reach his "heaven." These steps include the quick sale of the company to Dick Prospect for "forty crisp notes." Shortly thereafter some of this money is used to hire an English lawyer, Frederick Ashley Ring, to defend Gabriel in court, an arrangement that reduces Crystal's anxiety about her son's future. Thus Fox, finally free of all obligations except the one he desires with Crystal, is now ready to live his dream but this dream becomes a nightmare.

The early moments of episode six in act two, the jolting denouement joining the Aristotelian peripety (reversal) and anagnorsis (recognition) in this drama of sustained irony, show Crystal and Fox reveling in their dream-become-reality. We first hear them offstage as they move down the road of life towards the archetypal crossroads with signs pointing in four directions ("the hub of the country") on a beautiful sunny day. Chattering, laughing, whooping and singing like "happy children", they reach the crossroads with Fox carrying the rickety gambling wheel, the accordion and the stove and Crystal lugging two shabby suitcases. Fox also carries a bottle of wine which he shares with his wife, important symbolic action indicating that the Fox has, indeed, claimed his grapes but in liquid form.

Convinced that "their immediate worries have been solved", both Crystal and Fox are "elated", and Fox is especially "jaunty and vivacious", behaving like a young man "being flamboyant to entertain and impress his girl." Thus the journey back through time seems to have been completed successfully, a time-tripping flight from the circumscribing present followed by a seemingly magical metamorphosis that transforms the taller Crystal into a young maiden and the wrinkled, middle-aged Fox into a jaunty young man. Insisting that they are going to spend the rest of their lives "here in the middle of nowhere" (the glimpsed, timeless realm of joyful adolescence), Fox exclaims: "This is the life, girl, it should have always been like this."[9]

Vigorously exerting himself to maintain this extended self-deception, a mood of "controlled recklessness" suggesting a triumph over time, Fox pleads with Crystal to "marry me, again", a request which reveals his confused and desperate desire to repeat the memorable moments of their past. Yet Crystal is unable to behave perpetually like the impulsive young woman so active in Fox's memory -- the forthright, barefooted companion of the road. Understandably the Crystal has become clouded and corroded with the fissures of tragic self-awareness, an awareness joining accusation, guilt, anxiety and fear, and so Crystal gives her husband his first glimpse of her true, inner condition in this speech:

> I am not drunk, Fox. But I am rotten. Papa's dying in a hospital. Gabriel's going to jail. The show's finished. We've no money. And I'm happy as a lark. Amn't I rotten, my Fox?[10]

Crystal continues to surprise her husband and to erode and erase his comfortable, unexamined conception of her as a guileless, compassionate companion incapable of machinations when she informs him that she was aware from the outset of his acknowl-edged plans to wreck the company by driving away all of its members:

> You did, my love. I know you did. And I never under-stood why you did those things. I wondered, of course, 'cos I know you loved him. But I never understood. And maybe I didn't want to know, my Fox, because I was afraid -- it was the only fear I had -- I was terrified that you were going to shake me off, too. And I didn't really give a damn about any of them, God forgive me,

not even Pedro, not as long as you didn't turn on me.
That's all I cared about. And now we're back at the
start, my love; just as we began together. Fox and
Crystal. To hell with everything else.[11]

Momentarily stunned by Crystal's confession which brings her
inherent, disguised selfishness to the surface, Fox can only
stare at his muddied Crystal with "utter amazement and incredu-
lity." Recovering his composure, he briefly interrogates his wife
before jolting her with the disclosure that he betrayed their son
Gabriel to the police so that he could collect the one hundred
pounds reward money offered for his capture, an impulsive lie
that sends Crystal running from his side in sobbing frenzy:

> What ... are ... you? (He puts out a hand to touch her.
> She recoils and screams.) Don't -- don't -- don't ----
> don't touch me! (She backs away from him.) Get away
> from me! Don't come near me! Don't touch me! Don't
> speak to me! Don't even look at me! Must get away from
> you---evil ... a bad man ... It's too much ... I don't
> know you[12]. Don't know you at all ... Never knew ...
> never ...

Agitated by the lie which has just alienated his wife, a lie that
entered his head "a few minutes ago" and one that he could not
repress, Fox then explodes with a candid, impassioned confession
about the vision that set his destructive scheme in motion:

> Lies, lies, yes, I wanted rid of the Fritters and Billy
> Hercules, yes, I wanted rid of Cid and Tanya, and I
> wanted rid of the whole show, everything, even good
> Pedro, because that's what I saw, that's the glimpse I
> got the moment the fog lifted, that's what I remember,
> that's what I think I remember, just you and me as we
> were, but we were young then, and even though our
> clothes were wet and even though the sun was only
> rising, there were hopes -- there were warm hopes.[13]

Yet he quickly follows his confession with the melancholy admis-
sion that he chased after his vision because love was not "enough
at all, not nearly enough" to sustain and inspire him anymore. He
had lost his early buoyancy, falling into a prolonged disenchant-
ment that gradually deepened into despair. He changed from a
jaunty young man into a tormented, ruthless, older man with a
dream -- into an "autistic" (the term the psychiatrist used to
define his son), a person "unable to respond emotionally to
people." Hence he drives all of his associates, his son, and his
wife from his side, and we see him, confused and terrified,
admitting near the end of the play that "I don't know where I'm
going or what will become of me."[14]

The Wheel Has Come Full Circle

Bewildered and relatively incoherent, he ends the play by mocking
himself in a long, disjointed speech as a wise man who "knows all
the answers" because he had "learned the secrets of the universe"
where everything is "fixed." Viciously spinning his gambling
wheel, he invites imaginary customers to place their bets on red,
yellow, black or blue, chanting in his fairground voice: "You
pays your money, and you takes your chance."[15] Yet he undercuts
his apparent belief in the gambler's professed belief that riches
won at gambling will make you "happy for life" by asking: "But
who am I to cloud your bright eyes or kill your belief that love
is all?"[16] Hence this confused, terrified man obviously suspects
his cynical counsel and his presumptuous right to preach his
suspect wisdom, a wisdom that could dim the bright eyes of the
innocent and destroy the glowing faith of the young in love.

Isolating the traditional beast fable as the model which will
provide him with certain stock figures, animals, scenarios,
properties and moral ideas, Friel then selects what he needs for
Crystal and Fox, discarding and rearranging some of his raw
materials to meet his larger objective: the construction of a
dark, ironic fable about a man destroyed by his impossible dream.
He retains the Fox as his protagonist but he identifies him with
a knight on a quest, a bike rider who would fit easily into a Sam
Beckett play and who, on his third attempt, finds, falls in love
with and marries a "princess" who remains his "constant enchant-
ment." The playwright also associates Fox with the father in the
Biblical story who welcomes the prodigal son, absent for five
years, with a vigorous embrace, but this embrace is misleading.
One devious Fox cannot tolerate another treacherous Fox, and so
it is Pedro, the substitute father figure in the play, who
provides (not the fatted calf) but a bottle of whiskey for the
homecoming celebration.

Friel also appropriates the simple song "A-hunting We Will Go"
from the folktale "The Farmer in the Dell" as the theme song for
his play, and the members of the troupe, linking arms so as to
perform a dance, sing this part of the song near the end of
episode one in act one:

> A-hunting we will go,
> A-hunting we will go.
> We'll catch a fox and put him in a box.
> A-hunting we will go.
> Tantiffy tantiffy tantiffy,[17]
> A-hunting we will go.

Thereafter Fox Melarkey is the only member of the cast to occasionally sing snatches of this song, snatches mocking the efforts of the others to entrap him. Occasionally he sings the refrain "A-hunting we will go" which hints at his compulsive, deep-rooted desire to continue his search for his grapes. Fox also sings part of the song about "a happy land far away where we get jam four times a day" after the defection of El Cid and Tanya, desertions that move him closer to his imagined paradise. Yet the members of the company are never able to catch the Fox and put him in a box. Ironically, it is the Fox himself who traps himself in an empty box, in a solitary life which may become increasingly unbearable because of his painful memories of past joys, machinations and destructive actions. So Friel's Fox, unlike the fox in the fable, does get his grapes but they prove to be not only "sour" but "rotten." The return to the roads with Crystal, coupled with the drinks of wine and the exposure to the sun which makes them "sun drowsy", relaxes Crystal's protective restraint and so she spontaneously confesses that she is selfish and insensitive, a disclosure that compels the Fox to see his wife in a different, negative way for the first time. Yes, he has changed, but so has his wife; the crystal has become clouded.

Hence Friel exploits folk material to fashion a dark fable about an acting company that habitually seeks out catastrophies (especially those like fires in orphanages that kill numerous children) which attract large crowds which will fill their tents, a dark fable and a complex collage that is decidedly Pinteresque in its sense of menace, puzzling dialogue, uneasy silences, abrupt shifts in movement and mood, larger, mythical patterns, evocative richness, and quick glimpses into the contradictory aspects -- the murky interiors -- of people who, like T. S. Eliot's J. Alfred Prufrock, have cultivated a talent for preparing a face to meet the faces that they meet. In harmony with its larger objective, Crystal and Fox does not introduce us to wagons loaded with humble pilgrims -- to nomadic, simple souls of spontaneous goodness often associated with a Wordsworthian world of clear lakes, green fields, winding lanes and glorious sunrises. No, the "princess" is a "vixen" and her husband is a "weasel" man of "depth", a talking machine and a mechanical man who admits that he is "perverse." Falling from innocence into suspicion and feverish, desperate restlessness, Fox surrenders to the hypnotic power of his powerful vision that lures him into a hell of disorientated despair. The play's final scene focuses on the despairing Fox, his face buried in his arms that rest on his gambling wheel. The foxy gambler has spun his Wheel of Fortune and lost: the wheel has come full circle and he is there: a shattered isolato beside the road of life.

Beckett's Older Odd Couple

> "My work is a matter of fundamental sounds (no joke
> intended) made as fully as possible, and I accept
> responsibility for nothing else."

Deirdre Bair, Samuel Beckett: A Biography

A much slower journey by another, much older married couple down
a different, uneven, dust-covered road providing access to a
small train station in rural Ireland is also the organizational
scheme for Samuel Beckett's All That Fall, a pessimistic, philosophical parable that suggests that life is, indeed, a painful
pilgrimage toward greater physical and mental discomfort and
death, a shuffling odyssey made less onerous by man's experimen-
tation with language and by his comical candor that enables him
to laugh at rare intervals at his fragile, finite, self-conscious
self and at the various fictions and philosophical systems that
falsify and distort the nature of existence. The train station
which Maddy Rooney (the pun in the name suggests vigorous mental
"madness" in a malfunctioning, physical ruin of a body) is
struggling to reach is named Boghill, the name revealing
Beckett's chronic fascination with polarities of all kinds. Again
Beckett seems to juggle several contraries in the play: Wet-dry,
low-high, dark-light, blindness-sight, backward-forward,
disintegration-reproduction, cynical despair-hopeful love -- and
this grating clash of antithetical orientations becomes more
pronounced as the characters (especially the Rooneys) converse.

A witty, observant, garrulous old woman weighing more than two
hundred pounds, Maddy, ignoring her heart and kidney trouble, is
determined to surprise her blind husband Dan when he returns in
the evening from his office in the city on this June day which is
his birthday. Passing a ruined house in which an unidentified
woman is listening to a recording of Schubert's "Death of a
Maiden", Maddy is overtaken first by Christy, a truthful cart-
driver, who tries unsuccessfully to sell her some dung, and then
by Mr. Tyler, a retired bill-server just out of the hospital, who
curses both man and God for "the wet Saturday afternoon" of his
conception. Rejecting Mr. Tyler's offer of assistance, Maddy
sends him away so that she may grieve in private for the death of
a maiden, her daughter Minnie, who would have been in her forties
had she lived.

Maddy's third encounter on her tiring journey involves Mr.
Slocum, one of her old admirers and clerk at the nearby racecourse who offers her a ride in his high-wheeled car with new
balloon tires. After an extended, farcical wrestling match that
is punctuated by the groans and grunts of both participants and
which forces Mr. Slocum to position himself behind the heaving,

old woman, Maddy is shoved/hoisted into the car, a comic sequence of sexual innuendo which identifies Mr. Slocum as a "dry old reprobate" slow to experience orgasm (the pun in his name) and Maddy as a sexually-satisfied female who is, nevertheless, worried about her husband's future reaction when "he feels the hole" -- the hole in her torn frock. After killing a hen, another death of a living female creature, Mr. Slocum and Maddy arrive at the station where Tommy, a porter, helps her extricate herself from the car, her exit comically associated with the emergence of an infant from the birth canal.

After some conversation with Mr. Barrell, the station master whose name (another pun) suggests a railway roundhouse, Maddy asks Miss Fitt, a social misfit often lost in her religious musings, for assistance in climbing the station's stairs which Maddy associates with the Matterhorn. Minutes later the mail train roars through the station, and it is followed, a few minutes later, by the late passenger train which deposits the blind Dan Rooney who, with stick in hand and assistance from the small boy Jerry, is reunited with his anxious wife Maddy. After "cooly" greeting his wife who asks if he is well, Dan and Maddy began the return journey to their home, a laborious task that enables the misanthropic Dan to discuss the pleasure he gets from mathematical calculations, his retirement plans, his fear of the Lynch twins (another pun) who pelt them with mud, his blindness and general ill health, his desire to become deaf and dumb, his recurrent wish to kill a child, especially the boy Jerry who leads him home from the station each evening, the horrors of home life and his hatred of his silent, back street, basement office which makes him believe that he is buried alive.

Odd Couple As Dante's Damned

After Dan suggests that Maddy walk on facing forward while he walks on facing backward like Dante's damned whose tears water their bottoms, Maddy remembers a lecture by a "mind doctor" about a little girl who died because, in the doctor's view, she had never been born, another maiden half dead while alive. This new, unorthodox alignment of Beckett's odd couple (Dan refers to them as the "perfect pair") is revelatory because it identifies Maddy as one who walks forward tenaciously confronting the hazards of life and it exposes Dan as one who turns his back on life, a cowardly complainer who selfishly depends upon his stronger partner for support and guidance. This grotesque arrangement also suggests that life is a hazardous journey through an earthly inferno of physical pain and mental anguish.

Yet Dan refuses to answer Maddy's questions as to why the train was fifteen minutes late, asserting that he knows "nothing".

Annoyed, Dan threatens to "shake" Maddy off unless she stops
asking questions. Later, abruptly shifting from "normal" to
"narrative tone", Dan begins to summarize the train's journey in
a long, puzzling "composition" which does not explain the cause
for the train's delay but which does disclose that when the train
stopped somewhere on the track during its normal thirty- minute
run, Dan paced between the seats "like a caged beast." After
laughing wildly at their discussion of the new preacher's text
for tomorrow's sermon -- "The Lord upholdeth all that fall and
raiseth up all of those that be bowed down" from Psalm 145 -- the
Rooneys are overtaken by Jerry who comes running after them with
an "object like a ball" which Mr. Barrell says Dan has dropped.
After first denying that the ball-object is his, Dan later admits
that it is a "thing" which he carries with him in his travels.
When Jerry starts back toward the station, Maddy stops him with
the question as to why the train was late. Jerry quickly tells
her that a child had fallen out of one of the carriages and had
been killed under the train's wheels. Shocked by Jerry's disclosure, Maddy can manage no reply -- one of the few instances in
the play when she is speechless -- and the play ends with only
the sounds of dragging feet and wind-rain tempest breaking the
silence.

A play designed to be broadcast on the radio but not performed on
the stage, All That Fall boldly rejects the visual in favor of
the auditory, first recording and then deliberately reducing
verbal in favor of nonverbal sounds, the sounds momentarily
establishing a provisional reality that quickly vanishes to be
ultimately replaced by a disconcerting final silence interrupted
only by a "tempest of wind and rain." Hence it is the play's
soundscape -- the cries of sheep, bird, cow and cock, at first
solo and then together, the music from a ruinous, old house, the
sound of tired, dragging feet, the ring of a bicycle bell, the
"murderous rattle" of a motor van, the final squawk of a crushed
hen, the roar of a high-wheeled limousine, the bells, whistles,
hissing steam and clanking couplings of a passenger train, and an
Irish chorus of human voices -- voices humming, cursing, sobbing,
screaming, groaning, laughing, describing, remembering and
interrogating -- that remind us of a musical composition. Ranging
from muted music and murmuring to cacaphonous crescendos, All
That Fall is a carefully contrived orchestration rising and
falling in acoustic space. Yet it is the chorus of intersecting
voices uttering cliches, ejaculations, invectives and narratives
with different objectives and with different cadences, levels of
precision and auditory pitch that creates the poetry in this
play, a melancholy, elegiac poetry recognizing universal decay
(falling leaves, ruinous houses, diseased people) in large,
alternating units of silence and sound distinguished by balance
and a rising/falling rhythm which is repeated and repeated.

Being less than half alive in an eroding, dissolving world where, as Maddy Rooney affirms, it is "suicide to be "abroad" and a "lingering dissolution" to remain at home, Beckett's walking wounded limp toward greater immobility and certain death, gazing straight ahead at what Mr. Slocum describes as "the void". Yet they do not go quietly or submissively into that dark night. No, they talk and they talk and it is their talk which defines and connects them and which makes their painful pilgrimage to the grave endurable. Indeed, their language imposes temporary form upon and extracts temporary meaning from the relentless flux that everywhere swirls about them, a flux that steadily reduces and erodes the sharp angles of individual identity into "big pale blurs" blanketed with white dust. So life is like being buried alive.

Like the apprehensive people in Matthew Arnold's "Dover Beach", Beckett's people move across "a darkling plain" in an apparently indifferent universe devoid of certitude, peace and satisfactory relief for pain. Consequently, like Arnold's couple, some of Beckett's solitary souls (especially Maddy) strive "to be true to one another." Using different levels of language for different reasons and with different degrees of competence, courage and candor, Beckett's world weary pilgrims struggle to maintain the precarious relationships with their mates and family members, to establish some fleeting, reassuring moments of compassionate contact with their fellow travelers, to blur or heighten the visible edges of an onerous reality and to amuse themselves at odd moments with mirthless laughter at the unhappiness so pervasive in a world where God does not intervene to reassure and rehabilitate all those who have fallen into leaf-clogged ditches or under the wheels of trains. So talk equals therapy for Beckett's people wandering in a vast void but because their words are ephemeral, falling quickly back into silence, they must go on repeating the verbal process. It is sound versus silence, vocabulary against the void.

Talk is certainly a habitual, challenging and creative, therapuetic process for Maddy Rooney, Beckett's "hysterical old hag" in her seventies who, despite her contrary opinion, has not been destroyed by sorrow, gentility, church-going, fat, rheumatism and childlessness. Like the old man pacing and raging against old age in William Butler Yeats' "The Tower", Maddy also has an "excited, passionate, fantastic imagination" and an eye and an ear for the shapes, colors and sounds of the real world. Glancing up at the changing sky, asking neighbors about their ill family members, listening to Venus birds cooing and lambs baaing as they did centuries ago in Arcady, laughing at her own sudden, uncontrollable impulses or at the eccentric antics of her fellow countrymen, Maddy is "never tranquil." A compassionate and tolerant woman bravely confronting and enduring the physical-mental pain

of old age, Maddy does not surrender permanently to despair.
"Seething" out of her "dirty old pelt" and "skull", Maddy finds
wild delight amidst sharpest woe, sometimes tearing at her
"cursed corset" as if she would free herself from chafing restric-
tions, her own personal limitations, from history and the flow of
time itself so as to be joined with the dance of the atoms.
Agitated, she would dissolve, losing her form in the ever-
recurring flux.

Yet while she has life and an altered, sagging human form (Maddy
advises Miss Fitt to look closely if she wants to discern Maddy's
"once female shape" under the layers of fat), Maddy must talk,
and it is her "bizarre" talk (she insists that she uses only the
"simplest words") that isolates her in this Irish company which
includes some expert equivocaters. As she admits after arriving
at the station, people gravitate toward her, people full of
kindness and anxious to help, but she "estranges" them all with
impatient requests for assistance and with her candid speech,
especially the latter. Consistently, her speeches, more varied
and concrete than those by the ten other voices in this radio
play, are distinguished by their natural, sometimes explosive
directness and force, by a syntax appropriate to the situation,
and by a vivid and vigorous versimilitude, by an admirable
fidelity to the subject being described or discussed. She
repeatedly speaks with power and precision, refusing to use
language dishonestly to camouflage or conceal the pastoral beauty
or the pervasive misery in her world or to invent extended
fictions about the possibility of divine intervention in human
lives.

When Mr. Barrell mentions, for example, his father who died
shortly after his retirement, Maddy is quick to provide a prose
portrait of the dead man, describing him as a "small, ferrety,
purple-faced widower, deaf as a doornail, very testy and
snappy."[18]   Later, when she is exasperated with the dark Miss Fitt
for ignoring her to meditate about her Maker, Maddy explodes with
five quick expletives: "Your arm! Any arm! A helping hand! For
five seconds! Christ, what a planet!"[19] Still later, Maddy
becomes a landscape painter in prose, quickly sketching in the
milieu with loving exactness: "No. The entire scene, the hills,
the plain, the racecourse with its miles and miles of white rails
and three red stands, the pretty little wayside station, even you
yourselves ... and over all the clouding blue, I see it all."[20]

Maddy Annoyed with Equivocaters

With her linguistic candor and concreteness, Maddy has little
patience with the equivocaters, with those who use euphemisms,
incorrect diction and sophisticated syntax to mask the truth they

refuse to acknowledge. For example, when Maddy asks Mr. Barrell why the train is late and he replies that all "traffic is retarded" because there has been a "hitch", Maddy replies derisively:

> Retarded! A hitch! Ah these celibates! Here we are
> eating our hearts out with anxiety for our loved ones
> and he calls that a hitch! Those of us like myself with
> heart and kidney trouble may collapse at any moment and
> he calls that a hitch! In our ovens the Saturday roast
> is burning to a shrivel and he calls that ---[21]

If Mr. Barrell makes communication difficult with incorrect diction, then the dark Miss Fitt annoys her listeners with her extended syntax, losing herself in the flow and swirl of words that insulates her -- like her Sunday religious musings -- from the imperfect world that refuses to go away. As Miss Fitt explains:

> Why even when all is over and I go out into the sweet
> fresh air, why even then for the first furlong or so I
> stumble in a kind of daze as you might say, oblivious
> to my coreligionists .... Ah yes, I am distray, very
> distray, even on week-days .... I suppose the truth is
> I am not there, Mrs. Rooney, just not really there at
> all. I see, hear, smell, and so on, I go through the
> usual motions, but my heart is not in it, Mrs. Rooney,
> but heart is in none of it .... So if you think I cut
> you just now, Mrs. Rooney, you do me an injustice. All
> I saw was a big pale blur, just another big pale
> blur.[22]

Thus Miss Fitt, who wanders through this world but is not of it, does not use language to communicate ideas and feelings that would connect her with others in the human family. No, she plays with language in a self-indulgent, egocentric game, her long talks with herself reminding one of interior monologues or incantations that induce trance-like states that shut out the realities of life, reducing them to "big pale blurs." It is language to cushion and console but not clarify and connect, and it sometimes causes its speaker to eat her doily instead of the thin, buttered bread.

Yet it is the blind Dan Rooney, the unloveable, embittered man as human calculator who wants to shut out or ward off external stimuli by losing his remaining senses, who stands forth as the puzzling, professional Equivocater in this play. A moody, mysterious man with murderous desires which he has had difficulty restraining all his long life, Dan uses language to alienate others and to protect himself; he does not wish to communicate and connect with others, but only to confuse and confound them. His evasive answer to his wife's questions about why the train was late (she asks him five times) is an elaborate fiction told in a "narrative tone", a long, disjointed narrative about the cost of train tickets, food, drink, tobacco, periodicals, hair-trims, shaves, rent, licenses and other items, the monotonous horrors of domestic and office rituals, and his nervous pacing on the train.

Apprehensive about the success of his narrative, Dan subsequently asks Maddy to "Say you believe me." Perhaps Maddy believes him (perhaps she has to believe him to preserve the relationship) but the play's listeners suspect this chronic complainer with a cane. Remembering Dan's earlier encounter with the Lynch twins when he admitted to a strong, recurrent desire to kill a child, listeners suspect that Dan's tale is an evasive action designed to conceal his involvement in the death of the child under the train's wheels. Perhaps Dan, pacing furiously on the stalled train, pushed the child from the compartment because, having lost his only child, he hates all other living children. Or perhaps he refuses to tell Maddy about the child's death because he wishes to shield her from the news of another child's death, perhaps another maiden, a compassionate ploy at variance with much of his earlier speech and behavior. The play's circumstantial evidence suggest that Dan is guilty of murder but the listener cannot be certain of what is true. As it is with other Beckett plays, All That Fall takes place in a dark, dissolving, ambiguous world where the only certainty is uncertainty.

If Maddy is troubled about her husband's involvement, premeditated or impulsive, in the death of the child, she does not reveal it in her speech or behavior in the remaining minutes of the play. No, she continues to converse with her husband, interrogating and consoling him and clinging to him with affection as the rain and wind increase in greater flow and force. After asking that Dan put his arm around her, Maddy joins in the "wild laughter" which she and her husband enjoy after Maddy repeats the new preacher's text for tomorrow's sermon, some black humor that scoffs at the idea that God "raiseth up all those that are bowed down." This moment of mirthless laughter, joining Beckett's odd couple in a brief moment of harmony, moves Maddy and she pleads: "Hold me tighter, Dan."[23]

Yet this harmony does not last because Jerry's arrival with the object that "looks like a kind of ball" and which belongs to Dan prompts the blind man to assert that "Perhaps it is not mine at all."[24] Then, when Maddy asks Jerry twice if he knows what the "hitch" was that delayed the train, Dan interrupts: "Leave the boy alone, he knows nothing."[25] Yet Jerry does know something and his last words about the child "Under the wheels, Ma'am", the

77

last verbal sounds in this radio play, push Maddy (and those listening in the audience) into a meditative silence that may last for several hours or days. Alone with her irascible husband and her thoughts, Maddy will continue her halting return to her home and her "comfortable bed" where she may decline "slowly painlessly away" while "remembering ... all the silly unhappiness of life" as though it had never happened. Yet she will keep up her "strength with arrowroot and calves-foot jelly" and with her talk therapy, the voice of the hopeful humanist who knows that a "little love, daily, twice daily, fifty years of twice daily love" is what one needs to sustain her/him in his often painful journey through life.

Maddy certainly manifests a love and chronic concern for others, especially the suffering women in this world, as her questions following her encounters with others show. Shortly after meeting Christy, she asks him about his wife and daughter who are "no better" and "no worse"; Maddy then asks Mr. Tyler about his daughter and he discloses that she has had a hysterectomy, an operation that is to leave him, like Maddy, grandchildless; and she asks Mr. Slocum about his "poor mother" and his reply indicates that they are only able to "keep her out of pain." Maddy can't ask Tommy about his family because he is an orphan, and she does not ask Mr. Barrell about his immediate family members but she does remember Mr. Barrell's father because he was one who lost a maiden to death, his wife. Later, Maddy admits that she would not have "importuned" Miss Fitt had she known that the latter was searching for her mother, the wise Maddy knowing full well that Miss Fitt is one dazed drifter who needs all the assistance she can get in her groping progression through the labyrinth of life. After the train arrives with her husband Dan, Maddy changes her question and asks Jerry about his "poor father"; she is told that he has been "taken away", presumably to decline and die. Yet Maddy returns to her concern for the afflicted women in this world on her return journey, sympathizing with Mrs. Tully who is beaten by her husband and with the "very old woman" listening in her "great empty house" to "Death of the Maiden", the music that introduces one of the play's major concerns and that serves as a framing device for the play's sequence.

A Sly Fox and A Mysterious Man

Using the same structural strategy -- the journey down the road of life by two married couples -- Friel and Beckett introduce us in Crystal and Fox and All That Fall to two Irish odd couples who, though manifesting some dissimilar traits, are quite similar in several respects, especially the men. Friel's Crystal is much younger and more physically agile than Beckett's Maddy but both are clear-eyed, articulate observers of life. Less of a teasing talker than Maddy, Crystal is a selfish survivor, a duplicitous actress who lacks Maddy's tolerant affection for every living creature. Like Maddy, Crystal shows concern for her only child, a migratory man who survives, until he is arrested, by stealing and committing acts of violence. Like Maddy, Crystal is also lovingly loyal and faithful to her treacherous husband, and she severs their long relationship only when she is driven into hysterical frenzy by her husband's lie that he has betrayed their son for some pieces of silver.

Despite his advanced years, ill health and blindness, Beckett's Dan Rooney has much in common with Friel's sly Fox. Both are arbitrary, anti-social schemers, devious conspirators who are tired of traveling and who detest the daily routines that burden their lives. Mercenary and stingy, they are both cost-conscious, careful planners and opportunists who use and abuse others, especially their wives. Finally both Dan and Fox are professional liars, experienced, expert talkers who use words -- not to clarify issues and thereby establish contact with others -- but to mask their intentions and to conceal truths that would expose them to moral censure. Beckett's blind Dan is not, however, as unfortunate as Friel's Fox; he does not lose his wife on this June day that is progressively filled with "the encircling gloom" mentioned in the hymn which Miss Fitt hums and Maddy sings.

Two realistic plays, one a rewritten fable and the other a parable and serious comedy, Crystal and Fox and All That Fall remind us that disappointments are numerous and that disease and death are unavoidable in life. Certainly both plays cause us to reflect about the hazards related to impossible dreams and idiosyncratic whims and visions that transform men and women into social misfits -- into treacherous exiles and introspective drifters. Friel's Fox struggles to repeat the past, wrecking his company, his marriage and his life in the process; Miss Fitt ignores all others in her long dialogue with her Maker; and Dan disregards Maddy to calculate costs and to dream of an escape to a painless haven. Possessing a tolerant wisdom extracted from woe, Maddy Rooney is different from her fellow Irish travelers. Steadily plodding onward through this small world that fairly hums with different kinds of machinations and mathematics, Maddy is Beckett's "hysterical old hag" and heroic humanist who reminds us that laughter and love, the first inadequate and the second impossible, are acts of courage that momentarily dispel the silence and the solitude in a world where people know that they are "far from home" and lost in the "encircling gloom."

CHAPTER SIX

PRELUDE

The Beginning of the End of Gaelic Language and Culture

Following the Act of Union in 1801, the liberals in the English
government initiated a series of programs designed to integrate
with greater precision the affairs of Ireland, especially
economic and cultural affairs, with those of the United Kingdom.
In 1829, the English government passed the Catholic Emancipation
Act, an act allowing for minor changes in the land possession and
voting rights of the Catholic peasantry in Ireland. Yet it was
still illegal at this time for these same Catholics to attend
religious services or to receive formal education. Thus the Irish
Catholics had to keep their language and cultural traditions
alive by attending classes in caves, open fields and barns. In
due time these illegal assemblies became known as hedge-schools.

To maintain these schools the peasant families in a community or
region would arrange for an impoverished scholar to teach their
children how to read and how to use mathematical tables, paying
the itinerant scholar with pennies and farm produce—eggs, milk
and vegetables. Often the level of instruction was low but at
some happy intervals some communities would succeed in attaining
a scholar with a knowledge of the classical languages (Latin and
Greek) and the basic subjects. Irish novelist William Carleton
disclosed that he studied Saint John's Gospel in Greek when he
was attending one of these hedge-schools at age fourteen.

Fearful that these classes in Gaelic inspired and nurtured Irish
nationalism, the English government reacted in the 1830's to
erase this Gaelic legacy. In 1830 the English officials
authorized an ordnance survey of Ireland, and soon English
surveyors were swarming across the Irish countryside with their
tripod instruments and Name Books, altering both the spelling and
nomenclature of local place-names. Frequently difficult Irish
place-names were simply replaced by English equivalents. Then in
1831, the English government established the national school
system, and English was to be the only language of instruction in
these new schools. Within a decade 3,500 of these schools were
situated all over Ireland, providing instruction in English for
some 400,000 Irish children.

This new English-imposed system of education, the first in
Ireland since the abolition of all Catholic church schools under
the Penal Code sanctioned by William III after his victory at the
Battle of the Boyne, quickly eroded and erased Ireland's Gaelic

culture. In 1833 the population of Ireland was eight million and almost ninety percent of these people spoke Gaelic. Yet by 1879, as a consequence of the great famine of 1845 and the national school system, only twenty percent of the population could still speak their native tongue.

Friel's Translations shows the impact of this ordnance survey and the compulsory educational system upon a typical Irish village, the townland of Baile Beag (Gaelic for small town), an impact causing unemployment, theft, flight, threatened evictions and violence. Tragically one method of public education stressing the study of the Gaelic, Latin and Greek languages is replaced by another with a sole concern for the English language, the language, as the play suggests, of commerce and progress.

Friel's Translations: the Ritual of Naming

> The naming of things has always been a magical act. The
> magic is, of course, an expression of power .... Every
> people seem to have some ritual surrounding the naming
> of a person. Naming is one of our crucial, distinctive
> powers. We attach our presence, our magic, to the
> things we name.
>
>   Michael Quigley, "Language of Conquest,
>   Language of Survival"

> In our age there is no such thing as 'keeping out of
> politics.' All issues are political issues, and poli-
> tics itself is a mass of lies, evasions, folly, hatred
> and schizophrenia. When the general atmosphere is bad,
> language must suffer.
>
>   George Orwell, "Politics and the English Language"

The major issues are political, the general atmosphere is bad,
very bad indeed, and language does suffer in Brian Friel's
Translations (1981), a three act play recording the erasure/
replacement of one language and culture, Gaelic, by another,
English. Located in a hedge-school in the townland of Ballybeg,
an Irish-speaking community in County Donegal in Northern Ireland
in late August, 1833, the play traces the different responses--
silent, comic, romantic, belligerent, drunken and tragic--which
schoolmaster "Big Hughie" O'Donnell, his two sons, and their
scholars make to the English encroachment into their native
region, an encroachment signaling the closing of their hedge-
school and an invasion involving a large number of English
soldiers and some "sappers" or surveyors who have been assigned
the task of making a new map for--not just the region---but the
entire country. The English successfully complete both of their
assignments, replacing the hedge-school with an English-
sanctioned "national school" (where English will be the only
language taught) to be built at Poll nag Caorach, and replacing
all the Irish place-names with new, standardized English ones, a
translating task which, surgically and tragically, cuts off the
natives from their culture--from their living geography, history,
mythology and literature--and leaves them stranded and apprehensive in a strange, new world with unfamiliar language labels.

This two-pronged English assault on this island colony, basically
a commercial venture designed to facilitate and accelerate to
maximum efficiency the flow of Irish goods and services down
Irish roads and rivers and through Irish intersections with new,
quickly recognizable English name tags, is designed to achieve

two objectives: to disassociate the Irish from their past and to control their future, a control deliberately linked to the immediate transformation of Irish topography and to the future educational process, especially the use of language. First, the British imperialists will perform a frontal lobotomy upon the village of Ballybeg and the rest of the country, instantly reducing the Irish to cultural illiterates, to tongue-tied children uncertain about their identities and the new road signs appearing everywhere. Then the British, controlling the school system, will write a new script upon the Irish tabula rasas, changing the disoriented Irish into English-speaking puppets, into bewildered, inarticulate workers surviving and moiling in still another of colonial England's market places.

Maire, the "strong-bodied" milkmaid who brings cans of milk to "Big Hughie" and his crippled son Manus who live in the loft of this school-barn, explains how different life will be for her Irish-speaking associates at the new national school:

> And from the very first day you go, you'll not hear one word of Irish spoken. You'll be taught to speak English and every subject will be taught through English and everyone'll end up as cute as the Buncrana people.[1]

Thus Friel's _Translations_ indicates that nineteenth century English empire builders, with an eye for long-range results, appreciated fully the importance of language in colonial enterprises, in the extended process of cultural conditioning designed to keep the natives tranquil and productive. Manfred Stanley also investigates the central role of language in twentieth century cultural conditioning in his _The Technological Conscience_, a brilliant book showing how technology often manifests ignorance regarding the nuances of language, and an instructive study of the universal complicity in the erosion of linguistic disciplines that literally lights up the major thematic aspects of Friel's play. Defining technology ("technicism" is his term) as a language turned to illegitimate ends, Stanley argues that education is, ideally, the means by which students are inducted into the responsible use of language, an induction which makes students reflective individuals aware of and capable of exercising intelligent freedom of choice over the various capabilities of all systems of thought and practice. So, for Stanley, to be educated is to be literate: "To be literate is to attend to the world around us; to interpret what we hear and see; and to name in our own voices the conclusions we are prepared to let inform our conduct."[2]

Yet Friel's Irish villagers, displaced persons in a familiar world suddenly become unfamiliar, can't yet name in their own voices their conclusions because they are people—bewildered

victims--facing the challenge of acquiring a new language.
Indeed, they are similar to Stanley's technological children,
those illiterate moderns who can't appreciate the nuances of
language and so are deprived of cultural memory, full individual
self-consciousness and freedom itself. So, in demonstrating how
nineteenth century colonialism and twentieth century technology
can produce tongue-tied, cultural illiterates, both Friel and
Manley isolate the dangers inherent in an educational process
designed primarily to serve commercial-technical objectives.
Participants in this myopic educational process are deprived of
those basic competencies--cognitive, linguistic and social--which
they must have if they are to achieve full selfhood in the larger
social world. And Stanley pinpoints the crucial political-moral
problem which Friel is musing about in Translations when he
writes about the need for a standard of "moral-linguistic
accounting" in public affairs: "We can no longer afford to allow,
as we are presently doing, agents of powerful institutions to do
anything they want with language, the most significant of human
symbolic phenomena."[3]

Lancey As Orwell's Official

The chief agent for a powerful institution in Translations is
Englishman Captain Lancey, a small, crisp, middle-aged officer
uncomfortable with people, who is determined to carry out his
orders and to protect British interests in Ireland. When invited
in Act I by Owen, "Big Hughie's" other son working as an
interpreter-translator for the English, to explain to the natives
his mission in Ireland, Lancey launches forth on a prolix and
pompous explanation that is weighted down with pretentious
diction, an explanation that reminds one of George Orwell's
assertion that political writing is often used "to dignify the
sordid process of international politics."[4] Momentarily intoxi-
cated by his own eloquence, Lancey then proceeds to read from
what he refers to as a "white paper" and "our governing charter,"
his pompous, mechanical manner reminding one of an unthinking,
obedient, career-minded political-military person programmed to
talk in hackneyed, ready-made phrases which anesthetize the
listener's mind. Orwell's description of the "tired hack" or
official on the platform mechanically repeating familiar phrases
is relevant here:

> One often has a curious feeling that one is not watch-
> ing a live human being but some kind of dummy: a
> feeling which suddenly becomes stronger at moments when
> the light catches the speaker's spectacles and turns
> them into blank discs which seem to have no eyes behind
> them. And this is not altogether fanciful. A speaker
> who uses that kind of phraseology has gone some

> distance towards turning himself into a machine. The
> appropriate noises are coming out of his larynx, but
> his brain is not involved as it would be if he were
> choosing his words for himself.[5]

Truly, Lancey does not choose the words for himself. Indeed, the
three parts of his speech which follow the introduction remind us
again of Orwell's observation that government officials are often
guilty of "gumming together long strips of words which have
already been set in order by someone else."[6] Lancey's assertion
that England's map-making project "cannot but be received as
proof of the disposition of this government to advance the
interests of Ireland" is a euphemistic lie. England is making the
map to advance her own, aggressive commercial interests and
Lancey's explanation, assembled "like the sections of a pre-
fabricated hen-house"[7], cannot mask this intent.

After Lancey's performance, the two brothers--the stylish Owen
and the crippled Manus--meet downstage to evaluate the English
officers and to discuss Owen's translations in one of the most
significant scenes in this play about the use and abuse of
language. Boldly accusing Owen of not "saying what Lancey was
saying", Manus provides his own translation of Lancey's remarks,
adding that the map-making project is nothing but "a bloody
military operation." Vigorously contending that there is nothing
"incorrect" about the place-names which the Irish have used for
centuries, Manus cries out against this English-sanctioned
"ritual of naming", a ritual based on the basic premise: "Where
there's ambiguity, they'll [the Irish words] be Anglicized."[8]
Alertly underscoring the dangers inherent in this name-changing
ritual, courageous Manus points out that the English have already
eroded Owen's identity, his sense of self, by changing, without
asking, Owen's name to "Roland." Mentally squirming to extricate
himself from Manus' relentless assault, Owen protests: "What the
hell. It's only a name. It's the same me, isn't it? Well, isn't
it?[9]

The obvious answer to Owen's two questions is, of course, "No, it
isn't the same me." He isn't Owen, the former teaching assistant
in the hedge-school and a scholar in love with three languages:
Irish, Latin and Greek; he is now a well-dressed, deferential
lackey, an employee in but one of many commercial enterprises
maintained by the English colonial system. His identity has been
altered and eroded by the arbitrary ritual of naming, and his
loss prefigures the larger loss which is to follow--the loss of
their historical-cultural identity by all the Irish people living
in this English colony, a colony being mapped, netted and tamed
by surveyors blind to virtually everything else except their grid
coordinates.

Ralph Waldo Emerson's speculations about language, especially the corruption of language, impose additional layers of meaning upon this Owen-Manus exchange. Indeed, Emerson's discussion of language in chapter four of his long essay "Nature" provides special, revelatory glimpses into the thematic core of Friel's play:

> The corruption of man is followed by the corruption of language. When simplicity of character and the sovereignty of ideas is broken up by the prevalence of secondary desires, the desire of riches, of pleasure, of power, and of praise,--and duplicity and falsehood take the place of simplicity and truth, the power over nature as an interpreter of the will is in a degree lost; new imagery ceases to be created, and old words are perverted to stand for things which are not; a paper currency is employed, when there is no bullion in the vaults. In due time, the fraud is manifest, the words lose all power to stimulate the understanding or the affection.[10]

The corruption of man is followed by--not the corruption--but the abolition of language in Friel's play. In Acts II and III Owen will discover that he has lost some of his Emersonian "simplicity" (honesty); his fondness for words and ideas has been eroded by "secondary desires"--the itch for English gold and recognition. So he has become committed to a task where, to alter Emerson's sentence, old words are totally erased and new words, English words, are "perverted to stand for things" which they cannot adequately represent. Thus Owen is helping to create a "paper currency", a currency totally divorced from the Irish "bullion" in the ancient vaults, and this new, standardized language will lose "all power to stimulate the understanding or the affections" of the resentful Irish.

Lost In A New Linguistic Contour

Ironically it is the Englishman Lieutenant Yolland, Captain Lancey's angular assistant in the map-making enterprise, who realizes that the Irish, as "Big Hughie" affirms, are being "imprisoned in a linguistic contour which no longer matches the landscape of fact,"[11] and he warns Owen that "something is being eroded" and that an "eviction of sorts" is taking place. Praising the astuteness that enables one "to adjust for survival", Owen ignores Yolland's remarks. Rather, after finally explaining to Yolland that his name isn't "Roland", Owen joins his companions in the poteen drinking near the end of Act II, a drinking "celebration" in honor of the ritual of naming, the "hundred christenings" and a "thousand baptisms" of the new names in this Irish

Eden. As Owen exclaims: "We name a thing and--bang--it leaps into existence."[12] Disporting himself like a drunken god naming aspects of his creation, Owen prolongs with poteen his self-deception, his refusal to confront his role as "go-between" in a venture more commercial than benevolent.

The play's ending demonstrates that Yolland's prediction has taken place and that the Irish are now exiles in their native land. "Big Hughie", near drunk after a long sojourn at a wake, returns to the hedge-school to examine the Name Book which his son Owen has prepared for the English, a "catalogue" of names that will enable the natives to "learn where we live." Insisting in his drunken musings that "it is not the literal past, the 'facts' of history, that shape us, but images of the past embodied in language", "Big Hughie" asserts that his countrymen "must never cease renewing these images" or they will "fossil-ize."[13] Yet Hugh's countrymen face an impossible task because the images of their past will vanish with the loss of their language.

Praising <u>Translations</u> as a "coherent, disciplined" play focusing on the "inalienable peculiarities of language and nationality", the "strata" of historical and familial identities embedded in Irish place-names, Michael Quigley argues that the play identi-fies language with history which, in Ireland, means the record of calculating British colonialism:

> Friel's text is a complex one...because his subject is the whole story of the long clash between two nations, two languages....In his opening remarks Captain Lancey declaims to the assembled villagers...that 'this survey cannot but be received as proof of the disposition of this government to advance the interests of Ireland.' The road to Empire is paved with such good intentions. But the play ends, as it must, with the removal of the velvet glove of disinterested cultural and scientific advancement and the naked application of military force. This is no more than a reminder of the integrity of the two faces of the Empire. Whether the instrument is the gunboat or Coca-Cola, the purpose and outcome remain the same.[14]

Ronald Bryden also agrees that <u>Translations</u> is a play about language:

> Brien Friel's play is about the language which embodied the Irish peoples' ancient intimacy with their land. The triumph of English, <u>Translations</u> implies, robbed Ireland of her memory, was the original sin which expelled the Irish from the Eden of their legendary past, deprived like Adam of the power to name their

87

world....Clearly, <u>Translations</u> is a play about
Ireland's present griefs, the griefs, Friel suggests,
of a people struggling to rediscover a lost identity
and wholeness, to say who they are. For the traditional
symbol of Kathleen ni Houlihan, he submits the figure
of the tongue-tied peasant girl Sara, unable to name
herself to herself.[15]

Yet Bryden also realizes that the play's larger implications move
it far beyond the problems which are specifically Irish and into
the international arena of alienated, modern man living in a
world he knows all too imperfectly:

> The very nature of modernity is alienation from the
> old, live bond between land and people, soil and
> culture, which language once enshrined. As Orwell
> warned, language is the bedrock of justice. Tamper with
> the just fit of words to things, and you destroy the
> just fit between man and his world, between man and
> man. As language becomes more international, standard-
> ized, unlocalized, it loses fitness and precision, and
> with them we lose our power to name our place in the
> universe....We become colonialized people with artifi-
> cial identities imposed from elsewhere, which cannot
> fit our reality.[16]

Defining words as signs of natural facts, Emerson also identified
language as that vital creative process that enabled man to live
in harmony with nature--the Me and the Not Me--and to glimpse his
place in the larger universe. Pointing out that every word used
to express a moral or intellectual truth was "borrowed" from some
material appearance, Emerson praised the honest and eloquent man
who, accepting the radical correspondence between visible things
and human thoughts, conversed in a "picturesque" language distinguished by its concreteness and its "figures":

> As we go back in history, language becomes more pictur-
> esque, until its infancy, when it's all poetry; or all
> spiritual facts are represented by natural symbols. The
> same symbols are found to make the original elements of
> all languages. It has moreover been observed, that the
> idioms of all languages approach each other in passages
> of the greatest eloquence and power. And as this is the
> first language, so it is the last. This immediate
> dependence of language upon nature, this conversion of
> an outward phenomenon into a type of somewhat in human
> life, never loses its power to affect us.[17]

Emerson subsequently linked man's language to his integrity: "A
man's power to connect his thought with its proper symbol, and so

to utter it, depends on the simplicity of his character, that is, upon his love of truth, and his desire to communicate without loss."[18] Thus Emerson would find the British conquerors in Friel's Translations decidedly deficient in "simplicity" of character. Their love of truth is restricted to British commercial truth and they (notably Captain Lancey) lack the ability (or the strong desire) to connect their thoughts to the proper symbols; they do not really want to "communicate without loss." Thus the British invaders, with the imposition of the new language, tamper with the just fit of words and people to things and places, an arbitrary action condemning the Irish and themselves to an extended period of exile and alienation in a new world that is not so brave.

Owen Is the Judas Figure

Yet the major flaw in this play about the use and abuse of language is traceable to Friel's inadequate development of the character and career of Owen O'Donnell, the intelligent and responsive schoolmaster returning to the region that had shaped him but returning as a capable and willing worker for the English, the empire builders with a need for maps. Ignoring Owen's psyche as a potential battlefield for the conflicting forces, Friel does not provide enough episodes that show Owen's growing awareness of his Judas-like actions, the betrayal of his friends for pieces of silver. Owen seems to believe that the unexamined life is worth living because his basic guide for action is a "you go along to get along" philosophy. You adjust and survive and succeed.

It is Manus, the clear-eyed brother, who sees the patterns of history repeating themselves in the village, and he points out, at the beginning of Act III, that "There are always the Rolands, aren't there?" to complete the tasks assigned to them by powerful invaders, Viking, Norman or English. The one moment which suggests that Owen has some misgivings about his work occurs late in Act III near the play's conclusion. He is carrying a large stack of books across the school room and the Name Book falls from the top of the stack. He then stoops to retrieve the book, hesitates, and then leaves, disappearing from sight up the stairs leading to the living quarters of the hedge-school. This brief scene, embryonic to be sure, seems to suggest Owen's symbolic rejection of the Name Book, the directory which he has compiled in aiding and abetting the enemy and which reminds him of the Irish place-names he has killed with his translations. Yes, the book is properly named, giving the names of those killed and discarded in this confrontation of cultures.

One additional episode even closer to the play's end causes additional speculation about Owen's future conduct. After tossing a sack over his shoulders to protect him from the rain, Owen informs his father that he is momentarily leaving the school because he has "got to see" Doalty Dan Doalty. Perhaps Owen has serious issues to discuss with Doalty, the emerging rebel, who earlier told Owen that the Irish should "all stick together" in reacting to the impending crisis involving the slaughter of cattle and the eviction of people from their homes. Subsequent Irish history discloses that Owen and Doalty—and many, many others—did "stick together" in confronting the invaders' threat to their freedom and well-being.

Chapter Seven

Quick Glances Backward: Some Cross-Pollination of Irish Plays
and Paintings

> "Patterns contain the nature of nature."
>
> Soetsu Yanagi, The Unknown Craftsman

This brief book is arranged as a critical collage (some black
lines assembled in small units on flat, white paper surfaces)
about another larger and more complex collage--eleven plays by
six modern Irish playwrights--which might be likened to panels
in a national mural or to speaking paintings in a national
museum. This larger collage both joins and juxtaposes certain
basic raw materials, some large geometric patterns, some vibrant
colors, and some different textures and motifs--some muted and
others strident--in subtle and dramatic configurations. Distinguished by pluralism, both in theme and design, this large collage
is irradiated in some sequences by a technical audacity, by a
theatrical transcendentalism which attempts to break away from
and to rise above the traditional formalism of earlier realistic-
representational-rhetorical plays.

The two plays of Chapter One-- O'Casey's The Plough and the Stars
and Johnston's The Scythe and the Sunset--suggest splashes of
brilliant red against a drab grey-green canvas in a vibrating
patchwork that is taut with tension and which projects a texture
that asks to be touched--a gritty, angular versimilitude of faded
wallpaper, ragged articles of clothing of many colors, chipped
and broken crockery and dark deposits of stale tea. While
Johnston's play cracks at time with cerebral energy, certain
gnomic and aphoristic lines blazing forth like strips of colored
tape on metal surfaces, O'Casey's play embraces, stabilizes and
synthesizes swirling pools of color and motion as animated figures
leap, twist and collide in the narrow spaces that threaten their
romantic aspirations--a vivid vortex that pushes the viewer
toward momentary vertigo. Apprehensive people menaced by powerful
political, economic and religious forces--this is the situation
which also occurs in Within the Gates, Cock-A-Doodle Dandy and
Translations.

We must change the colors to bright greens, yellows, purples,
oranges and browns in Within the Gates and Cock-A-Doodle Dandy
and we must also move beyond pictorial art with these two ritual
plays because they are, in many respects, plays for dancers.
With large casts of characters limping, marching and sprinting
through a criss-cross network of irregular curves, these two plays,
especially Within the Gates, approach ballet. Exploiting places
many-layered with memory and association, O'Casey stands forth

as the restless, poetic visionary in these two plays, manifesting
a glittering eclectic virtuosity that blends archetypal figures,
ritual, song, dance, symbols and natural settings which hint at
some reciprocal penetration of outer and inner worlds, the raw
and often cruel present with the historic-mythic past.

Camille Souter's painting "And So Came Spring"--an abstract work
with two circular patterns--reminds one of the seasonal cycle in
O'Casey's park-play, and Tony O'Malley's "Studio Window, Summer"--
with its dark wall, dark red, sinking sun, numerous vivid flowers
and brilliant blue sky--successfully evokes the Act One, vanishing
splendor of Nyadnanavé in Cock-A-Doodle Dandy. Using the window
motif so dear to the Romantics to organize his painting, O'Malley
expresses his delight with the natural world, allowing the outside world to impinge upon the inner world of the artist's studio.
As viewed through the upper-level window in his twisted, sagging
and sinister black house, Michael Marthraun's garden and surrounding
landscape beyond his stone fence could have looked in the opening
moment of the play like O'Malley's very vivid painting.

Brian Bourke's "Winter" is, in many aspects, the pictorial equi-
valent of the bleak worlds created by Yeats in Purgatory and Beckett
in Krapp's Last Tape, the two plays in Chapter Three. With a
severe suggestiveness that rivals the dialogue of Yeats and Beckett,
Bourke's painting reproduces with realistic accuracy a building,
some bare trees and the grounds surrounding the building which could
be the old man's house before the fire in Purgatory. Blending
the sombre mauves of remembered winters with the grey zones of
the present winter, this painting suggests a reality filtered
darkly through the lens of memory. Moreover, the roadway in the
foreground of "Winter" hints at wider vistas and possible involvement with life, motifs that remind us of the roads not taken by
Beckett's Krapp. Yet it is Louis Le Brocquy's "Isolated Being",
an abstract, faceless human figure (its outer contours eroded and
misty and its inner areas pitted with dark spots) in a light grey-
white world of isolation, that best captures the essence of Beckett'
Krapp's Last Tape.

Norah McGuiness's "Tide Receding, Dublin Docks", with the finger-
like buildings of Dublin in the background and some large, circular
patterns reflecting buried debris (and buried memories), can be
associated with Charlie Tynan's numerous trips in and out of Dublin
in Da. Dan O'Neill's "Knockalla Hills, Donegal", a rural scene
done with lush greens and light browns, could be associated with
the outskirts of the small village which Friel visits in Philadelphia Here I Come and Translations.

George Russell's "The Potato Gatherers" depicts the solid world of
daily toil through which Friel's Crystal and Fox and Beckett's
Maddy and Dan journey, a world with a dark earth and radiant sky.

Yet Basil Blackshaw's "The Field" is a more suitable pictorial
representation for the two plays, especially All That Fall. With
long, vertical brush strokes flowing from the foreground toward
a distant ridge that almost touches a low sky, "The Field" conveys
the impression of a slow, uneven movement through an oppressively
enclosed world toward an elevated ridge, a journey not unlike
that taken by Maddy and Dan in Beckett's dark universe.

Perhaps painters would define Friel's Crystal and Fox and Beckett's
All That Fall as dramas of linear arabesque where a few expressive
motifs--an old woman in a ruined house or a small circle of brooding
people around a campfire--appear against a backdrop of stark,
simplified planes and shapes. Certainly Friel uses the lower,
dourer range of the color spectrum in his world which is not far
removed from something primitive and sinister while Beckett, in
All That Fall, is a long way from his later paring down process--
the depersonalized theater of abstract word play and involved,
cerebral gymnastics, the drama of pure sounds and silences.

An impressive collage of different shapes, colors and moods with
its own diversified calligraphy, these eleven Irish plays indicate
that a playwright's style--his technical strategy--is conditioned
by his subject and by the physical-cultural world through which
he moves. Responding to historical lines of force, to the visual
culture all around him and to their own inner genius, these dramatists strive at times to fashion a new theatrical transcendentalism,
using images, colors, lines, angles and stage constructs that
will enable them to glance at the mysterious areas of the human
psyche disturbed by an often violent, external world where "things
fall apart". In specific scenes these writers seek a new, higher
level of luminosity and the woven complexity of an oriental rug
or tapestry to express their visions. Using a striding silhouette,
ghosts from the past, both male and female, an alter ego in human
form, recorded voices from the past, transparent, geometrically
grotesque houses, angular platforms, myriad colors, chanted speech,
diverse musical compositions and rituals known by many people,
these playwrights create concrete dramatic works which are vividly
visual, perhaps knowing (as Delacroix contended) that painting,
with its concrete language, is more suggestive than music.

Notes
Chapter One

[1]*Theatre and Nationalism in Twentiety-Century Ireland*, ed.
Robert O'Driscoll (Toronto, 1971), p. 104.

[2]See "Ideas and Ideology in *The Plough and the Stars*," The
Sean O'Casey Review, II (Spring, 1976), 126.

[3]Denis Johnston, *Collected Plays*, I (London, 1960), p. 4.

[4]*Ibid*., p. 10.

[5]*Ibid*., p. 67.

[6]*Ibid*., p. 68.

[7]*Ibid*., p. 97.

[8]*Ibid*., p. 11.

[9]Sean O'Casey, *Three Plays* (New York, 1973), p. 140. O'Casey
remembers the great affection among the Volunteers and the I.C.A.
men for colorful uniforms, especially the uniform worn by the
Volunteers of 1782, a resplendent uniform blending green, yellow,
red and blue colors. See *Drums Under the Windows* (New York,
1960), p. 337.

[10]*Ibid*., p. 185.

[11]*Ibid*., p. 196.

[12]*Ibid*.

[13]*Ibid*., p. 197. Explaining Clitheroe's conduct, Robert
Hogan contends that Jack continues to fight only "because he is
too afraid and too ashamed to give up." See Hogan and Sven Eric
Molin, *Drama: The Major Genres* (New York, 1962), p. 457.

[14]*Ibid*., p. 204. Describing the unveiling of the I.C.A.
flag, which Clitheroe and his comrades expect to carry into
battle, O'Casey mentions the "rich poplin field of blue" the
formalized shape of a plough, "a golden brown color, seamed with
a rusty red", and the group of stars "ennobling the northern
skies." *Drums Under the Windows*, p. 342. W. I. Thompson argues
that Jack desires the "glory" that comes with an officer's role
in the Citizen Army. See *The Imagination of an Insurrection* (New
York, 1967), p. 210.

Notes
Chapter One

[15]Letter to this writer from O'Casey, March 30, 1959.
Observing that detectives were in the Abbey Theatre audience on
May 3, 1928 to prevent the disruption of O'Casey's controversial
play, Joseph Holloway comments: "It was sad to think that a play
that offends many who love their country sincerely should be
protected by the police." See Joseph Holloway's Irish Theatre, I,
eds. Robert Hogan and Michael J. O'Neill (Dixon, 1968), p. 34.

[16]Johnston, p. 9. Reacting to the charge that he is an
"intellectual playwright", Johnston concedes that perhaps his
plays "deal with ideas too much, and too little with character."
See Gordon Henderson, "An Interview with Denis Johnston," The
Journal of Irish Literature, II (May–September, 1973), 33.

[17]Ibid., p. 94.

[18]O'Casey, p. 184.

[19]Johnston, p. 4. Observing that Irish playwrights are
generally "myopic" about women, Johnston adds that the Clitheroe
relationship presents a "false picture" because "It's the women
who usually drive the husbands into violence." Henderson, p. 31.

[20]Ibid., p. 48. For details about the real Endymion see
chapter one of Oliver St John Gogarty, As I Was Going Down
Sackville Street (London, 1980), pp. 1–9.

[21]Ibid., p. 5.

Notes
Chapter Two

[1] O'Casey discloses that the Messenger's name was "given to me by the well-known song 'ROBIN ADAIR.'" He adds that "the play's title was suggested by George Cohan's 'Yankee Doodle Dandy.'" Letter to this writer from O'Casey, October 28, 1963.

[2] Alluding to Ritual Culture Drama, Jessie L. Weston states that the main objective of these primitive dramas was "that of encouraging, we may say, ensuring, the fertility of the Earth." From Ritual to Romance (New York, 1957), pp. 28-29.

[3] Describing Within the Gates as O'Casey's most "comprehensive achievement," G. Wilson Knight views the play as one deriving its tension from "a number of ritual conflicts." The Golden Labyrinth (New York, 1962), p. 378.

[4] O'Casey, Collected Plays, Vol. IV (New York, 1964), p. 156.

[5] Ibid., II, p. 140.

[6] Ibid., p. 231.

[7] Ibid., p. 214.

[8] Ibid., IV, p. 218.

[9] Ibid., p. 222.

[10] See Bill Jack Harman and Ronald G. Rollins, "Mythical Dimensions in Within the Gates," Philological Papers, XVI (November, 1967) 72-78.

[11] Sir James G. Frazer, The Golden Bough, one-volume ed. (New York, 1940), pp. 140-141; see also The New Century Classical Handbook, ed. Catherine B. Avery (New York, 1962), pp. 170-174.

[12] Collected Plays, II, p. 137.

[13] Ibid., p. 147.

[14] Ibid., p. 130.

[15] Ibid., p. 127. Jessie Weston suggests that the king suffered "from infirmity caused by wounds, sickness, or old age." Ritual to Romance, p. 20.

[16]Bobbie L. Smith, "Satire in O'Casey's Cock-a-Doodle Dandy," Renanscence, XIX (1967) 64-66.

[17]Collected Plays, II, p. 227.

[18]O'Casey comments at length on the historical-symbolic significance of the cock: "The Cock has been for thousands of years a symbol of rising, of virility, of courage, of outspokenness - its crow is clarion: the herald of the dawn....Oh, I thought it plain by the context of the play that the COCK meant life, energy, alertness, courage. This fowl is a world symbol, familiar to Shakespeare. It is a symbol for France. It is the 'bird of dawn'; the 'herald of the morn', and, according to Shakespeare, when Christmas came, it 'sang all the night through.' At one time it was believed that an effigy of the bird protected a home or building from evil - hence the weather-cock or weather-vane." Letters to this writer from O'Casey, October 2, 1959, and October 28, 1963.

[19]"From 'Within the Gates,'" The New York Times, October 21, 1934, Section 9, p. 3.

[20]Letter to this writer from O'Casey, July 25, 1959.

[21]See my article "Clerical Blackness in the Green Garden," The James Joyce Quarterly, VIII (1970) 65-75.

Notes
Chapter Three

¹The Collected Poems of W. B. Yeats (New York, 1959), p. 240.

²The Collected Plays of W. B. Yeats (New York, 1966), pp. 432-433. Peter Ure observes that Yeats gives us in the Old Man a "mixed nature" agitated by "criminality and his instinct to redress it." See Yeats (New York, 1963), p. 104.

³Ibid., p. 435.

⁴Ibid., p. 436. Alex Zwerdling explains Yeats' fascination with the real and the supernatural worlds in this passage: "To put the matter succinctly, the idea of an actual world intersected at innumerable points by a spiritual one appealed to Yeats because it raised the actual world to an ultimate level, while at the same time it created an opportunity for ecstatic visionary experience which did not leave man's world behind." See Yeats: A Collection of Critical Essays, ed. John Unterecker (Englewood Cliffs, 1963), p. 243.

⁵Leonard E. Nathan, The Tragic Drama of William Butler Yeats (New York, 1965), p. 243.

⁶Donald R. Pearce, "Yeats' Last Plays: An Interpretation", English Literary History, XVIII (March, 1951), 171.

⁷Collected Plays of W. B. Yeats, pp. 431-432.

⁸Pearce, p. 172.

⁹Ibid., p. 173.

¹⁰Collected Plays of W. B. Yeats, p. 430.

¹¹Ibid., pp. 435-436.

¹²Nathan, pp. 245-246.

¹³The Collected Poems of W. B. Yeats, p. 185. Joseph Holloway records his response to Yeats' play when he first saw it on August 10, 1938: "I was present at the Abbey for the first performance of W. B. Yeats' play in one act, Purgatory....Yeats' play was the story told by an 'old man' to his son outside the ruined house....It was a strange story of murder to rid the world of crime-makers: the old man killed his father and during the play's progress slays his son with the same knife. He is an old

Notes
Chapter Three

man haunted by memories...." Joseph Holloway's Irish Journal, III
(Dixon, 1970), pp. 11-12.

[14]Samuel Beckett, Krapp's Last Tape and Other Dramatic
Pieces (New York, 1960), p. 24.

[15]Samuel Beckett: An Autobiography (New York, 1978), p. 175.

[16]Ibid., p. 406.

[17]Ibid., pp. 350-351.

[18]Beckett, p. 22.

[19]Ibid., p. 24.

[20]Ibid., p. 25.

[21]Personality (New York, 1980), p. 25. See also Valerian J.
Derlega and Louis H. Janda, Personal Adjustment: The Psychology
of Everyday Life (Glenview, 1981), pp. 10-11.

[22]It is illuminating to compare Yeats' ideas in Purgatory
with the similar sentiments in this verse from "The Old Stone
Cross" in Collected Poems of W. B. Yeats, p. 314.

> Because this age and the next age
> Engender in the ditch,
> No man can know a happy man
> From any passing wretch;
> If Folly link with Elegance
> No man knows which is which,
>> Said the man in the golden breastplate
>> Under the old stone cross.

Notes
Chapter Four

[1] Brian Friel, *Philadelphia, Here I Come* (New York, 1965), p. 12. D.E.S. Maxwell contends that "The logic of the play is not in plot contrivance or 'what-happens-next', but in its delicate montage of past and present experience and feeling." *Brian Friel* (Lewisburg, 1973), p. 63.

[2] *Ibid.*, pp. 40-41.

[3] *Ibid.*, p. 43.

[4] *Ibid.*, pp. 91-92.

[5] *Ibid.*, p. 108.

[6] *Ibid.*, p. 109.

[7] *Ibid.*, pp. 110-111.

[8] *Ibid.*, p. 44.

[9] Hugh Leonard, *Da* (New York, 1978), pp. 11-12.

[10] *Ibid.*, p. 17.

[11] *Ibid.*, p. 49.

[12] *Ibid.*

[13] *Ibid.*, p. 50.

[14] *Ibid.*, p. 21.

[15] *Ibid.*, p. 41.

[16] *Ibid.*, p. 26.

[17] *Ibid.*, p. 28.

[18] *Ibid.*, p. 78.

[19] *Modern Drama* ed. Otto Reinert (Boston, 1966), p. 585.

Notes
Chapter Five

[1] Brian Friel, Crystal and Fox and The Mundy Scheme (New York, 1970), p. 40.

[2] Ibid., p. 41.

[3] Ibid., p. 35.

[4] Ibid., p. 68.

[5] Ibid., p. 69.

[6] Ibid., p. 29.

[7] Ibid., p. 102.

[8] Ibid., p. 123.

[9] Ibid., p. 127.

[10] Ibid., p. 136.

[11] Ibid., p. 137.

[12] Ibid., p. 144.

[13] Ibid., p. 145.

[14] Ibid.

[15] Ibid., p. 146.

[16] Ibid.

[17] Ibid., p. 25.

[18] Samuel Beckett, Krapp's Last Tape and Other Dramatic Pieces (New York, 1960), p. 52.

[19] Ibid., p. 57.

[20] Ibid., p. 61.

[21] Ibid., p. 65.

[22] Ibid., pp. 55-56.

Notes
Chapter Six

[1]Brian Friel, Translations (New York, 1981), p. 23.

[2]Manfred Staley, The Technological Conscience (New York, 1978), p. 221.

[3]Ibid., p. 251.

[4]The Little, Brown Reader, ed. Marcia Stubbs and Sylvan Barnet (Boston, 1983), p. 350.

[5]Ibid., pp. 354-355.

[6]Ibid., p. 353.

[7]Ibid., p. 349.

[8]Friel, p. 38.

[9]Ibid.

[10]Ralph Waldo Emerson, Nature and Other Miscellanies (New York, 1922), pp. 22-23.

[11]Friel, p. 51.

[12]Ibid., p. 54.

[13]Ibid., pp. 80-81.

[14]Michael Quigley, "Language of Conquest, Language of Survival," Canadian Forum, (November, 1982), pp. 14-15.

[15]Ronald Bryden, "The Dual Vision of Brian Friel," Program Notes for the Canadian Premiere of Translations at the Avon Theatre, Stratford, Ontario, July 12-September 2, 1982.

[16]Ibid.

[17]Emerson, pp. 22-23.

[18]Ibid.

Notes
Chapter Five

[23]Ibid., p. 82.

[24]Ibid., p. 88.

[25]Ibid., p. 89.

[26]Ibid., p. 90.

SELECTED BIBLIOGRAPHY

Allen, James Lovic. Yeats' Epitaph: A Key to Symbolic Unity in His Life and Work. University Press of America, 1982.

Bair, Deirdre. Samuel Beckett: A Biography. Harcourt Brace Jovanovich, 1978.

Barnett, Gene A. Denis Johnston. Twayne Publishers, 1978.

Bushrui, S. R. ed. A Centenary Tribute to John Millington Synge, 1871-1909. Colin Smythe, 1979.

Coh, Ruby. Just Play: Beckett's Theatre. Princeton University Press, 1980.

_____. ed. Samuel Beckett: A Collection of Criticism. McGraw Hill, 1975.

Ellis-Fermor, Una. The Irish Dramatic Movement, 2nd. ed. Metheun and Company, Ltd., 1954.

Harper, George Mills. The Mingling of Heaven and Hell: Heats' Theory of Theatre. The Dolmen Press, 1975.

Hogan, Robert. After the Irish Renaissance. University of Minnesota Press, 1967.

Kleinman, Carol. Sean O'Casey's Bridge of Vision: Four Essays on Structure and Perspective. University of Toronto Press, 1982.

Krause, David. The Profane Book of Irish Comedy. Cornell University Press, 1982.

Mercier, Vivian. The Irish Comic Tradition. The Clarendon Press, 1967.

Rollins, Ronald. Sean O'Casey's Drama: Versimilitude and Vision. University of Alabama Press, 1979.

Sahal, N. Sixty Years of Realistic Irish Drama. The Macmillan Company, 1971.

Taylor, Richard. The Drama of W. B. Yeats: Irish Myth and the Japanese No. Yale University Press, 1976.

Thompson, William I. The Imagination of An Insurrection. Oxford University Press, 1965.

Worth, Katharine. The Irish Drama of Europe from Yeats to Beckett. Humanities Press, 1978.